WHO
SWITCHED
THE PRICE
T GS?

Tony Campolo

A search for values in a mixed-up world

WHO SWITCHED THE PRICE TAGS?

WORD PUBLISHING

Word (UK) Ltd
Milton Keynes, England

WORD BOOKS AUSTRALIA
Heathmont, Victoria, Australia
SUNDAY SCHOOL CENTRE WHOLESALE
Salt River, South Africa
ALBY COMMERCIAL ENTERPRISES PTE LTD
Scotts Road, Singapore
CHRISTIAN MARKETING LTD
Auckland, New Zealand
CROSS (HK) CO
Hong Kong
EUNSUNG CORP
Seoul, Korea
PRAISE INC
Quezon City, Philippines

WHO SWITCHED THE PRICE TAGS?

ISBN 0–85009–110–1

Reproduced, Printed and Bound in Great Britain for Word (UK) Ltd, by Cox & Wyman Ltd, Reading.

This book is dedicated to

Norman H. Maring,
a teacher who is like a father,

and to

George Homsher,
a student who is like a son

ACKNOWLEDGMENTS

I want you to know a few people who helped me write this book. First, there is Beverly Carlson who did my proofreading and initial editing. She knows how to spell and how to write things in a way that is grammatically accurate. Without her, who knows what this book would be like? Second, there are my secretaries, Mary Noel Keough and Kimberlee Feeser, who did the typing. Without them, this book never would have gotten to the publisher. Finally, there is Pat Wienandt, my editor at Word Books. Without her, what I wrote never would have gotten into print. I thank these four people not only for their good work, but for their patience and caring. Now let's get on with discovering the value system that makes living a lot of fun.

CONTENTS

A VERY SHORT INTRODUCTION TO A VERY IMPORTANT SUBJECT

This book is about having fun. There isn't anything frivolous about having fun. Learning how to have fun is one of the most serious subjects in the world.

Without fun, marriages don't work. When jobs aren't fun, they become intolerable and dehumanizing. When children aren't fun, they are heartbreaking. When church is not fun, religion becomes a drag. When life is not fun, it is hard to be spiritual.

People don't know how to have fun. Often, they force themselves to do things that are supposed to be fun, but frequently they end up with a hollow feeling instead of the euphoria they expected to experience. They put on the faces of happiness as they consciously present themselves to one another at cocktail parties; yet, in unguarded, pensive moments, their faces sag and their expressions spell deadness and ennui. When you ask them how things are going, they say, "Couldn't be better." But you sense that perhaps they couldn't be worse.

I call this condition "the Peggy Lee syndrome." You may remember that Peggy Lee was the pop singer who once belted out a song entitled "Is That All There Is?" Her song asked the question that I think many people in today's world ultimately ask. A lot of people, after finally acquiring what they think they want in life, then find that this "heart's desire" fails to deliver the gratifications promised. The Buicks are not "something to believe in." The Pepsis do not give them "life." The Löwenbräu beer does not bring them "good friends." Somehow, life is supposed to be better. Somehow, they are supposed to be having more fun.

Once when I was in Disneyland, I saw a woman shaking her little boy and screaming at him, "You wanted to come, and now you're going to have fun whether you like it or not!" It seems to me that too many people are just like that little boy. They are supposed to be having fun, but they feel like crying. It does no good for them to force themselves to have fun. Having fun can't be forced, but it *can* be learned.

Getting the Price Tags Right

If we want to get the most out of life, we must learn to give priority to those things that are really important. Too often, we miss out on the best that life has to offer because we are distracted by what is of little consequence while ignoring that which is most deserving of our time and energy. The father who is too wrapped up in his job to spend time playing with his daughter may discover too late that he wasted his chance to enjoy one of this world's most gratifying experiences. The mother who is so busy keeping her house in order that she allows no opportunity for roughhousing with her little boy may one day realize she missed out on the laughter that makes having a little boy a precious thing. The couple who decide that they must "get ahead" even if it means they accept working hours that keep them from times of intimacy may discover too late that, in their pursuit of the American dream, they let something far more precious die. It is easy to undervalue what makes life joyful and to overvalue what eventually proves to offer little, if any, personal gratification. All too easily we get our value systems mixed up and then become confused about what delivers the *fun* that God wants us to enjoy.

When I was a boy in Philadelphia, October 30 had special significance. The night before Halloween was designated as Mischief Night. On that night, the adults of our neighborhood braced themselves against all sorts of petty "crimes" at the hands of the younger generation. Windows were soaped, air was let out of tires—all the annoying mischief an adolescent mind could conjure up we did.

One year, my best friend and I devised what we thought was a brilliant and creative plan for mischief. We decided to break into the basement of the local five-and-dime store. We did not plan to rob the place (Sunday School boys would never do that sort of the thing);

instead, we planned to do something that, as far as the owner of the store was concerned, would have been far worse. Our plan was to get into that five-and-dime store and *change the price tags* on things.

We imagined what it would be like the next morning when people came into the store and discovered that radios were selling for a quarter and bobby pins were priced at five dollars each. With diabolical glee, we wondered what it would be like in that store when nobody could figure out what the prices of things really should be.

Sometimes I think that Satan has played the same kind of trick on all of us. Sometimes I think that he has broken into our lives and changed the price tags on things. Too often, under the influences of his malicious ploy, we treat what deserves to be treated with loving care as though it were of little worth. On the other hand, we find ourselves tempted to make great sacrifices for that which, in the long run of life, has no lasting value and delivers very little gratification. Sometimes I think that one of the worst consequences of being fallen creatures is our failure to understand what really is important in life.

So many of us do not know *how* to have fun. How can we, when we do not even know what is important or what delivers a fun time? How can any of us have a good time in life when we ignore the things God has designed to deliver His joy? How can we know happiness if we give our lives to the things He warned would only make us sad?

If we are to be fun people, we must get our values clarified. We must put first things first. We must give attention to those things that foster good family life, satisfying work patterns, positive church life, and viable personal relationships. We must give our time and energies to those things that God teaches us to value, and construct our styles so we organize our lives around those things essential to life as He wills it to be lived. In other words, if we are to get the most out of life, we have to get our values straightened out.

How do we do that? In the following pages, I'll show you.

How This Book Is Put Together

This book is divided into four sections. In the first section, I want you to join me for some values clarification—looking at today's values, and seeing why they don't work. I will demonstrate how many of the young people of the 1980s have bought into a value system that won't deliver the fun that they long to enjoy. Their value system is anti-Christian, and I'll discuss why, and then offer a better and more Biblically based value system in its place. I believe that there is little fun for people who don't know what is really important in life. Fulfillment comes from spending time and energy on what is really significant. Therefore, I want, first of all, to clarify what *is* significant in life.

An erroneous value system is increasingly dominating our culture. This book provides an alternative system that will insure the joyful pay-off people long for in life.

The second section is designed to help people have fun at their jobs. I would like people to view employment as more than a way to make money. Work should enhance our humanness and leave us elated with life. If we work for the right reasons and if we enter our jobs with the right attitudes, such things can happen. And best of all, I believe that God wants such things to happen.

Family life is the subject of the third section. Every year in America, one million teenagers run away from home. Life at home may not always be easy, but children should feel that, regardless of the difficulties they experience, their parents are fun to be with. I'm going to do my best to explain how to make family life better and to show some ways that I think can make living at home more fun.

I'm also going to devote a great deal of discussion to marriage. Recently, I watched an elderly couple who were having pizza at a Pizza Hut near my home. They were having such a good time with each other that other people in the restaurant couldn't take their eyes off them. As I watched this couple, I thought about how few marriages offer the fun that those two people were having. For a great many Americans, marriage turns out to be a real drag. I hope that what I have to say helps people to enjoy their marriages more.

The last section of this book deals with church life. Most kids don't like going to church because they think it's a bore. Many adults go to church more out of a sense of duty than out of a sense of joyful expectancy. All in all, churchgoing is not as much fun as it ought to be. Not many people are saying on Sunday mornings, "I was glad when they said unto me, 'let us go unto the house of the Lord.'" I'm going to do my best to explain how to enhance the joy of being part of the church. Worship should be a celebration, and unless it is a celebration, it is not the kind of worship that God wants it to be.

Now that I've set the course, let's get on with the trip. Give me a chance to give you some directions into a fun-loving existence, because *fun is one very important consequence of true spirituality.*

Part One

CLARIFYING OUR VALUES

THE END OF THE AGE OF AQUARIUS

They are different than they used to be.
. . . The college students that I teach in the 1980s are far removed in attitudes and values from the ones I taught in the '60s. In the '60s, students seemed to be imbued with an idealism that was both naïve and challenging. They wanted to end racism, sexism, poverty, and war, and they wanted to end all of these things by tomorrow morning. They joined in endless marches for social justice and were convinced that, if they went to Washington and demanded that things be different, they would be. After all, they had grown up getting everything else they had demanded.

The collegians of the '60s were believers in a neo-

Marxist ideology that committed them to ending the alienation and the oppression which they believed were creations of "the establishment." Conservativism was a bad word to them. In their minds, a conservative was a racist, militaristic, chauvinistic pig. They called themselves "liberals" and felt that anyone who rejected their agenda was inhumane.

There was something that was both arrogant and likable about them. They seemed to have a secular value system that was more akin to the Sermon on the Mount than the traditional ideology of the mainline churches. They believed in the goodness of people and had the simplistic idea that evil was almost completely structural (i.e., it was the fault of flaws in the organization of society). They were convinced that the new era of social justice, ushered in with a placard here and a sit-down strike there, would release the underclass and allow them to become self-actualized, compassionate people. They were arrogant because they were convinced that they alone were the enlightened ones and that no one over thirty could be trusted. Their parents, they declared, were indoctrinated with a filthy materialism which their guru, Charles A. Reich, in his book *The Greening of America*, called "consciousness two." They were convinced that they represented the vanguard of a new mind-set which had outgrown the commercialized world of Madison Avenue advertisements and had taken on a higher form of human thinking which Reich named "consciousness three."

In this new society, which they were sure they could create in a decade or two, individualistic self-seeking and personal power-plays would be shed like outgrown knickers. In place of the egoistic lifestyles of the competitive, laissez-faire capitalism of America, theirs would be a communal lifestyle in which each would work generously according to his/her ability and each would receive according to his/her need.

I liked the outlook of these children of the "age of Aquarius." While they were arrogant and haughty, they did seem to have the right kinds of dreams. As a matter of fact, in their idealism I found values that I wished were more evident in the churches I attended and served. There was something noble about their visions of the future, and those of us committed to a radical theology of the Kingdom of God began to think that these young people were more Christian than most of those who filled the pews of churches. It was easy for religious types like me to be seduced by this emerging youth subculture of the 1960s. Those long-haired males and braless females possessed a childlike innocence that made them seem exceedingly fit for the Kingdom of heaven.

Of course, history attests to the fact that they were not quite as altruistic nor as committed to a new era of justice as they appeared to be. Sociological studies give evidence that their revolutionary fervor was more of a myth than a reality. But that makes no difference, because if things are real in the imagination, they are real in their consequences. Those of us who stood behind the rostrums of Ivy League universities in that hectic decade saw before us a generation of visionaries and dreamers who longed for a better world.

The youth culture of the '60s has become a dim memory of a never-never land that many of us can hardly believe really existed. When I talk now about the events and happenings of the '60s to my present students, I feel that I am talking about something that happened "once upon a time." The march on Selma, the collegiate outbursts following the intrusions of U.S. troops into Cambodia, the quixotic campaign of George McGovern, and the protest songs of Pete Seeger are not part of the brave new world of the business major types who more and more dominate the halls of the Ivy League.

In 1976, after ten years at the University of Pennsylvania, I left and have since dedicated most of my energies to teaching at Eastern College, a small Christian liberal arts school in Pennsylvania. I have established myself on a Christian college campus because it is one of the few places where enthusiastic idealism is still very much alive. Those students who are endowed with the Biblical message still give evidence of a commitment to challenging the evils of this world. With a longing for justice that flows from a personal relationship with Jesus, many evangelical students still cringe at the oppression and sufferings of the socially disinherited. Whereas the idealism of the 1960s proved to be a fad that dissipated in the face of the inflexibility of the American socio-economic order, the idealism of Christian college students seems to still be alive and well. Perhaps this idealism thrives in them because it is rooted in an eternal mandate that is as old as the Old Testament prophets and as new as the compassion imparted by the Holy Spirit.

While Christian students at both Christian colleges and secular institutions still speak of commitment to changing the world into something better, it seems that the secular students of our present decade have left such dreams behind them. They have pragmatically sought vocations that could offer them power, prestige, and most of all, wealth. They think that they can find satisfaction in such things. And that is their great mistake.

The New Generation as Viewed by *Fortune* Magazine

On April 7, 1980, *Fortune* magazine carried an article entitled "On a Fast Track to the Good Life." The article gave the findings of research done to clarify the values and attitudes of twenty-five-year-olds who were taking their places in the business world of the 1980s. The research was intended to give the readers of *Fortune* a brief thumbnail sketch of what to expect from young people during the next ten years. The study was most revealing. Allow me now to introduce you to this new generation of twenty-year-olds:

1. These young people believe that a successful life means financial independence and that the best way to gain financial independence is to be at the top of a major corporation.

2. They believe in themselves. They believe that they have the abilities and capacities to be the best. There is no "humble talk" among them.

3. They believe in the corporate world. They are sure that the corporations they would lead are the most worthwhile institutions in the world.

4. They view as "a drag on success" any relationship that slows their ascent of the corporate ladder. Marriage is an acceptable option only if it does not interfere with their aspirations for success. Having children, for most

of them, is something to which they will have to give a great deal of thought.

5. Loyalty is not high on their list of values. Unlike "The Organization Man," described by William Whyte, Jr., in his book of the same name during the '50s, the young Turks of this new breed have their resumés ever at hand. They are ready to move from one company to another and believe that loyalty to one company could lead to staying in a system that might not maximize upward mobility.

6. They are convinced that they are more creative and imaginative than those who now hold top corporate positions, and they believe that there is not much they can learn from these older types before they take their places.

When I read about these young people and their values, I felt sad and deeply troubled. I think Jesus would have said to them, "For what shall it profit a man, if he should gain the whole world, and lose his own soul?"* After reading the *Fortune* article, I was left with a sense that this new generation of young people would find most of the teachings of Jesus incomprehensible and that what they did understand, they would deem unacceptable.

The Beatitudes, as outlined in Matthew 5, are the antitheses of what these young people are all about. Jesus contended that those who become poor as they respond to the needs of others will be the happiest of people, but the "yuppies," the upwardly mobile young professionals of the 1980s, argue that happiness results from gaining financial success for self.

---

* Mark 8:36.

Jesus taught that those who are the happiest are those who are able to empathize with the sufferings of others. Students coming out of college these days tend to believe that happiness can best be found by focusing on their own well-being and not worrying about what breaks the hearts of those outside their personal world.

Whereas Jesus called meek people happy,* these young upwardly mobile professionals believe that happiness comes through a go-getting, success-seeking attitude which leaves little regard for loyalty to others.

Jesus' teaching about purity of heart must seem hopelessly naïve to the youth of the '80s.† They believe that everybody is out for "Number One" and that behind even the most altruistic behavior are motives that are oriented to personal gratification and sexual pleasure.

Their commitment to success at all costs makes them somewhat merciless towards those whose personal limitations prevent them from gaining a share in the American dream. They believe that people get what they deserve and those who fall by the wayside warrant little attention from those who have the talent and make the sacrifices essential for personal achievement. What Jesus says about being merciful‡ must seem to them like the kind of sentimentalism that gave birth to what they considered to be the useless and stupid give-away programs of President Lyndon Johnson's "Great Society."

Jesus told us that peacemaking brings happiness,§ but they are too committed to aggressively displacing their

---

* Matt. 5:5.
† Matt. 5:8.
‡ Matt. 5:7.
§ Matt. 5:9.

corporate superiors to pay much attention to such a thought. They believe in that Spencerian doctrine that the world is basically a jungle and only those who have the instinct to compete for survival are able to live in it.

The yuppie generation is interested in having good reports on their accomplishments. They want their résumés and their letters of recommendation to strengthen their position in the job market. They are not willing to be "persecuted for righteousness' sake." The idea of taking unpopular stands and opposing practices that reek of injustice seems foolhardy when such stands elicit negative responses from those in positions of power and influence.

They may go to church, but these contemporary yuppies are hardly the possessors of a Christian value system. Their successes may be a source of pride to their parents, but there is an anxiety among these parents that is not pleasant to behold. They repress a fear that when they are old, they will not be visited or tended to with much love by these upwardly mobile, tough-minded children.

A Word from the Wise Is Sufficient

Recently, I read a sociological study that has great significance for those of us who are trying to respond to champions of the yuppie value system. In this particular study fifty people over the age of ninety-five were asked one question: "If you could live your life over again, what would you do differently?" It was an open-ended question, and these elderly people were allowed to respond in unstructured ways. As you might imagine, a multiplicity of answers came from these eldest of senior citizens. However, three answers constantly re-emerged and dominated the results of the study. These three answers were:

1. If I had it to do over again, I would *reflect more.*
2. If I had it to do over again, I would *risk more.*
3. If I had it to do over again, I would *do more things that would live on after I am dead.*

I think that these elderly people have a good handle on what life is all about. I believe that their perspective gives better direction on how to live life with joy and satisfaction than we can gain from listening to the new kids on the block. Consequently, in the next three chapters of this book, we will explore the implications of what they are trying to tell us. I am convinced that people who want to have fun in life would do well to consider the observations of those whom time has made wise.

REFLECTING: GIVING MORE THOUGHT TO THINGS

The elderly people in the study realized in retrospect that they had not paid proper attention to the things in life that were of the greatest importance. They recognized that they had failed to appreciate properly many of the blessings that had been theirs by the grace of God. They sensed that they had not paid enough attention to the people who had been a major part of their lives. In short, they realized that they had not experienced life and all that it had to offer them with the depth and gratitude it deserved.

It is easy for us to nod with apparent understanding to their confessions. It is easy for us to hear them out and to respond with a patronizing, "Those old folks sure have something important for us to hear." Because what they have to say to us is so uncomplicated, we might be inclined to discount their insights, assuming that they are merely the quaint ideas of old people. Hopefully, this will not be the case. We can learn from these people who have become sages through ninety-five years of experience, and their thinking deserves our careful consideration.

Reflecting on the Grace of God

We Christians can easily explain what Jesus did for us on the cross. With relative ease, we can declare that the Son of God was put to death because of our sins. All too casually, we can point out that each of us is deserving of punishment from God, but that Jesus was punished in our place.

Time and time again, we have heard the story of how Jesus stood in our stead and endured the condemnation that each of us deserved for what we have done. The word "gospel" means "good news," and the good news is this: "There is therefore now no condemnation to them which are in Christ Jesus, who walk not after the flesh, but after the Spirit."° We are not condemned for one reason: because Jesus stood in our place and took upon Himself the condemnation and punishment that we deserve.

Whenever I make that kind of statement at a Pentecostal church, the congregation breaks into applause. They do so because they know how much Jesus deserves

° Rom. 8:1.

our cheers of appreciation. If we would stop to reflect on what He has done for us, we all would applaud Him—regularly.

While most of us know what happened on the cross, few of us reflect upon what Jesus suffered on our behalf. The hymn writer rightly tells us

> But none of the ransomed ever knew
>   How deep were the waters crossed;
> Nor how dark was the night that the Lord passed thro'
>   Ere He found His sheep that was lost.

I am convinced that if we reflected more about the pain and agony our sins brought upon Jesus two thousand years ago, our lives would be completely different.

During the Vietnam conflict, a young graduate of West Point Academy was sent to Vietnam to lead a group of new recruits into battle. He did his job well, trying his best to keep his men from ambush and death. However, one night he and his men were overtaken by a battalion of the Viet Cong. He was able to get all but one of his men to safety. The one soldier who had been left behind had been severely wounded, and from their trenches, the young lieutenant and his men could hear their wounded comrade moaning and crying for help. They all knew that venturing out into the vicious crossfire of the enemy would mean almost certain death. But the groanings of the wounded soldier continued on through the night. Eventually, the endurance of the young lieutenant came to an end, and he crawled out of his place of safety toward the cries of the dying man. He got to him safely and was able to drag him back. But just as he pushed the wounded man into the safety of the

33

trench, he himself caught a bullet in the back and was killed instantly.

Several months later, the rescued man returned to the United States, and when the parents of the dead hero heard that he was in their vicinity, they planned to have him come to dinner. They wanted to know this young man whose life was spared at such a great cost to them.

On the night of the dinner party, their guest arrived drunk. He was loud and boisterous. He told off-color jokes and showed no concern for his suffering hosts. The parents of the dead hero did the best they could to make it a worthwhile evening, but their efforts went unrewarded.

At the end of that torturous visit, the obscene guest left. As her husband closed the door, the mother collapsed in tears and cried, "To think that our precious son had to die for somebody like that."

That soldier owed those parents the best that was in him. It was evil for him to give so little thought to what they had lost because of him. Considering the price that had been paid for his life, his ingratitude was beyond comprehension.

But, before we go too far in our criticism of that ungrateful soldier, shouldn't we consider how much like him most of us are? Jesus died for *us*, yet we continue to sin. Jesus paid a terrible price to give us life eternal, yet we continue to behave obscenely. We owe Him something better, but we fail to deliver what we should. *We fail to reflect upon the cost of our salvation.* If we did our lives would be radically different.

The suffering of God did not end with Calvary. The sins we commit here and now bring pain to Jesus here and now. While the price paid for our sin was once and for all, our ongoing sin brings ongoing pain to our Lord. If we reflected upon what He endures daily because of what we do daily, we would be driven to turn from sin and, with zeal, live more righteously. In Hebrews 6:6 we read: "If they shall fall away, to renew them again unto repentance; seeing they crucify to themselves the Son of God afresh, and put him to an open shame." This verse reminds us that, not only did Christ agonize because of our sin when He was nailed to the cross, but that even now when we sin, we give Him pain and suffering. If we would only reflect upon how much our sin hurts Jesus, we would give it up. I know a woman whose husband pays her little attention. Her children are grown up and out of the house. She has little to do that gives her a sense of significance. For several years, she had become increasingly jittery about her self-worth and had become so depressed that she considered suicide. Then, unexpectedly, while serving on the building committee of her church, she got to know a young widower. This new man in her life found her interesting, treated her as though she were still physically attractive, and made her feel alive again. Not surprisingly, this relationship developed into an extended extramarital affair.

When she told me about her lover, she evidenced no remorse or guilt. She explained that her husband was extremely detached from her and had not responded to her pleas for intimacy for years. She reported that her children had moved thousands of miles away and seldom contacted her. She told me that she and her lover were very careful about their meetings and that there was almost no likelihood of their being found out.

"He makes me feel wonderful about myself and I help to meet some of his needs," she told me. "Nobody's hurt. Nobody suffers."

"What about Jesus?" I responded. "Do you ever think that what you are doing causes Him to suffer?" I went on to explain that I believed that Hebrews 6:6 teaches that when she commits adultery, Jesus goes through pain as intense as that which He experienced when they drilled the nails through His hands and feet two thousand years ago on Calvary. This woman's sin was psychologically tolerable to her only because she did not *reflect* more on the suffering of Jesus. Reflection would have driven her to repentance.

The Apostle Paul wrote in Philippians 3:10: "That I may know him, and the power of his resurrection, and the fellowship of his sufferings, being made conformable unto his death." Paul reflected often on the suffering that his sins brought on Jesus and, undoubtedly, that reflection motivated him to greater righteousness.

Reflecting on Glory

Sometimes, when life is overbearing, one of the few routes to joy we can find is in reflecting on our new standing before God because of Christ. Sometimes, when people around us make us feel like nothing, the best therapy we can find is in reflecting about how God sees us and what He has declared us to be before the angels in glory.

The Bible says in Romans 4:6 that God has imputed to us the righteousness of Christ, "Even as David also describeth the blessedness of the man, unto whom God imputeth righteousness without works." Quite simply, that means that we get credit for all the good things that Jesus ever did and God views us as being as wonderful as His Son. Not only does Jesus take our sin and make it His own, but He ascribes to us all the benefits for the good things that He has done, is doing, and will do. When I reflect on this, I often experience a psychic "high." I imagine myself someday bouncing into heaven and boldly marching up to the throne of grace to meet my Heavenly Father. If any angels stand in my way, I see myself saying, "Get out of my way, angels! I want to see my Father."

I don't have to be afraid of Judgment Day because all my sins are forgiven and forgotten. They are blotted out and remembered no more. When my Heavenly Father opens the Campolo book and reads about me, I haven't a thing to worry about. All the things in my life that are rotten and filthy, and all the things that are so shameful that I have never dared to share them with anyone, will be erased from my records. In place of all that garbage will be recorded all the magnificent things that Jesus did. The Bible says in John 2:25 that if all the things Jesus did were written down, all the books in the world could not contain them. And the incredibly good news is that all those things are "imputed" to me. When the Heavenly Father reads that list of good things, all my friends are going to say, "Hey, Campolo, did you do all of *that*?" I'm going to answer, "It's God's book! It's His book!" It's going to be fun to go to heaven.

The joy that comes from thinking about glory is a joy available to all who have surrendered their lives to Christ. All they have to do is just stop and *reflect* on it all from time to time.

Reflecting on Relationships

Every high school drama club, sooner or later, gets around to putting on Thornton Wilder's play *Our Town*. In the play, Emily, who is the main character, dies giving birth to a child. In the afterlife, the spirits grant her one wish, and she chooses the privilege of watching herself and her family live out one day of the life she left behind—she chooses her twelfth birthday. She watches herself and family as they talk and interact and carry on the ordinary activities of that day.

From her perspective as an invisible observer, she is shocked and dismayed by what she sees and hears. Neither she nor the members of her family seem to give serious attention to each other. Realizing how precious life is, she becomes angry because they are not emotionally involved in their interaction. They seem casual in what they say and do, not recognizing, as she does from the other side of death, that they will not have this day forever. She agonizes over the way the day transpires. She cannot stand to watch herself and her family waste what she knows to be infinitely precious time. She is shocked that they live life with so little reflection on its importance.

Then Emily turns on the audience and scolds us by asking, "Do any of you ever really live life while you're living it?"

The elderly people surveyed in the study mentioned earlier could understand Emily's pain. They were keenly aware of the fact that they had failed to reflect sufficiently upon their lives. They, too, had learned that the precious times we have with each other slip quickly by without our giving them the intensive attention which they deserve.

I am now fifty-one years old. Both my son and my daughter are grown up and out of the house. I know that, for the most part, they are out of my everyday life and I will never again see as much of them as I would like. But in my quiet times, I can recall those special moments when I stopped and allowed myself to feel their preciousness.

I remember one night, when my children were very small, and my wife called me into their bedroom. She pointed to them stretched out in their beds. Even now, I can see the angelic expressions on their faces and their peaceful innocence.

My wife whispered in my ear, "Look long and hard, Tony, because they'll never be like that again."

I wish I had done more such reflecting. I wish I had taken less for granted during our precious times together.

Reflecting on Self

I sometimes think that the way we teach our children to pray is all wrong. We teach them to pray, "If I should die before I wake. . . ." It would be far better to teach them to pray, "If I should wake before I die. . . ." Most people I know are so detached from life that they seem to be in a trance which renders them more dead than alive. And they sleepwalk their way through life without much awareness of the wonder of it.

The Apostle Paul calls us to have our "eyes wide open to the mercies of God . . . ,"* but most people only see "through a glass darkly." The elderly people in the study wished that they had paid more attention to life. They wished that their eyes had been more open to what many might call the simple pleasures of life. One old man who was interviewed said that he wished he had taken more baths and fewer showers. He said, "I just didn't spend enough time experiencing how good a hot bath really feels." These older people, if they had it to do over again, would give full attention to the color purple in violets and to the shades of blue in the ocean.

I can best describe what I mean with an illustration I've used in an earlier book.

While I was a faculty member at the University of Pennsylvania I taught a course entitled Existentialism and Sociologism. I would always start the semester by picking out some unwary student and aggressively asking him, "How long have you lived?" Usually, the student would be stunned into silence by the abrupt interrogation. Then I would press the student and ask a second time, "How long have you lived?"

The student, not sure what I was getting at, might answer, "Twenty-three!"

Then I would retort, "No! No! That's how long your heart has been pumping blood. I asked you, 'How long have you *lived?*'"

I would then go on to tell this story to illustrate what I meant by living:

When I was in the ninth grade, our class was taken to

* Rom. 12:10.

New York City on a class trip. Living just ninety miles away from "The Big Apple," our teacher found that city very accessible for school outings. Along with my classmates, I was taken to the top of the Empire State Building. I remember running around the viewing landing chasing somebody. (What else do ninth-grade schoolboys do on class trips?) Suddenly, I realized that *I* was on top of the Empire State Building. *I* was on top of the world's tallest building. I stopped chasing my friends and proceeded to enter into a state of wonder. In that magic moment, I was struck with the immensity of the city that lay before me. Slowly, I took a firm hold on the protection rail. Then, mystically, I took it all in. I experienced the city with an overpowering awareness. I stepped outside of myself and watched myself living and experiencing New York. I sucked in the scene. I lived what I saw with such intensity that, if I were to live a billion years, that moment would be part of who I am. That moment would be part of my "eternal now."

After telling the story I would return to the student and ask again, "How long have *you* lived?" I recall one student answering, "Well, when you put it that way . . . maybe a minute. Maybe two. Most of my life has been the meaningless passage of time between all too few moments of real aliveness."

Resurrecting a Dead Self

Most people I know are hardly alive at all, and those who are alive are truly alive all too seldom. This world that I inhabit is filled with people who are not so much characterized by sin as they are by deadness. In the words of C. S. Lewis, "Our age is marked by moderate vice and moderate virtue." It is the deadness of the souls rather than the perversity of souls that is the devil's most significant accomplishment on this planet. At least passionate sins are interesting. It is the death of the spirit evidenced among the so-called living that makes me desperately aware of how much the people of this world need the life-giving presence of Jesus in their lives.

In his poem "The Leaden-Eyed," Vachel Lindsay describes the deadness, the ennui, that plagues our generation:

> Let not young souls be smothered out before
> They do quaint deeds and fully flaunt their pride.
> It is the world's one crime its babes grow dull,
> Its poor are oxlike, limp, and leaden-eyed.
> Not that they starve, but starve so dreamlessly,
> Not that they sow, but that they seldom reap;
> Not that they serve, but have no gods to serve;
> Not that they die, but that they die like sheep.

As I reflect on my own life, I find that becoming a Christian has made me more alive to life and more aware of the wonder of existence than most people think possible. I do not hold myself up as a more virtuous person than others. I know many non-Christians whose lives give evidence of a morality that puts me to shame. However, what I do have going for me is *aliveness*. Since surrendering myself to being filled with the Spirit of Christ, I have an exuberant awareness of the specialness and wonder of life, and this awareness invigorates me wildly. Often, this exuberance expresses itself in ways that are seldom considered "religious" in a formal sense.

Yet, I believe that they are the essence of what religion is all about.

Clowning around is part of living just as much as crying is. I can accept both. What I cannot accept is that deadness in people which renders them incapable of either passionate joy or agonizing sorrow. What I cannot accept is a lifestyle that is "neither hot or cold."* The salvation offered by Jesus is much more than deliverance from hell and the promise of heaven. When Jesus offers us life, He offers it "more abundantly" here and now. Of all the blessings that God has to offer us in this life, none is more splendid than His indwelling, life-giving Presence. When I witness to people about what Jesus wants to do for them, I have much more to offer them than the promise of everlasting life. I can offer them a new quality of life in the present. I can assure them that, if they are willing to believe in Jesus and to commit themselves to being the kind of persons He wills for them to be, they can know life on a new level of joyful intensity. When persons say within themselves, "Jesus, I'll do what *you* want me to do and live how *you* want me to live," something wonderful happens. Jesus becomes a living Presence within them, and with that indwelling Presence, there comes an aliveness that equips such people to enter into life's experiences with passionate awareness. Jesus equips people to live with an intensity essential for appreciating what life has to offer. Jesus equips us to *reflect* on life and all that it has to offer "more abundantly."

* Rev. 3:15.

43

RISK-TAKING: THE STUFF THAT HEROES ARE MADE OF

When I was a boy growing up in Philadelphia, I loved to join my friends in playing a street game called "stick ball." In this game we used a broomstick as a bat with which we did our best to hit half a tennis ball. The game could be played by anywhere from two to a thousand players. Not surprisingly, whenever we played stick ball, we made a lot of noise and we frequently blocked traffic. That meant that the police would usually come and chase us away. Worst of all, the cops always took our sticks.

One day, we wanted to play stick ball, but much to our dismay, we had no sticks. Every broom within ten blocks of where I lived had been "raptured" by stick ball players, and then the cops had confiscated every one of them. These sticks were neatly stored in the back room of the police station, located at 55th and Pine Streets. We all knew where they were, but we didn't know what to do about it.

I remember sitting on a curb with some of my buddies bemoaning our sad plight and saying something I would have been better off not saying. I said, "Somebody ought to get into the back room of that police station where the cops store all those sticks they take from us and steal some of them back."

My best friend (who bore the nickname "Mush") then said in a sinister voice, "I dare you!"

When Mush said that, I reacted like a Pavlovian dog. Like a lot of boys, I had been conditioned to react to dares in ways that are hard to describe. My back would tighten. My blood would run hot. My heart would beat faster. All of this happened in response to the simple words, "I dare you."

"All right," I snapped. "You guys go into the police station before me, talk to those cops, and keep them occupied. Pretend that you have to do a term paper for school about police work. While you've got their attention, I'll get into that back room and I'll come out with five sticks—*or I won't come out at all!*"

I want you to know that the name Tony Campolo is still legend in West Philadelphia. The kids on the street still talk about the guy who robbed the police station at 55th and Pine.

Some kids get a thrill out of going to Disneyland. Others get excitement out of riding the roller coaster at the Magic Mountain amusement park. Some get turned on by surfing. But if you climb the highest mountain or zip down the tracks of the world's fastest roller coaster, you still won't know the exhilaration that comes from robbing a police station. I was on a high for three months! I was so pumped up with adrenalin that I bounced around for days like a jack ball.

Risk-taking is exciting. Risk-taking makes you feel heroic. Risk-taking gives you evidence that you are special. Risk-taking convinces you that you've got what it takes to break out of the mold which society casts for you. It is no wonder, then, that the elderly people surveyed in the study we've been mentioning claimed that, if they had life to live over again, they would risk more.

Looking back on life, these people didn't think much about their successes nor did they show much remorse over their failures. From the vantage point of old age, life's successes did not seem like such a big deal and life's failures did not appear to be the disasters they thought they were at the time they were happening. To the people who were 95 years of age and older, what seemed to matter were the risks they had taken.

Without Risks We're Stuck in Misery

There are people who have jobs that make them miserable but who won't leave them because they are afraid of the risks. Each morning, they make themselves go to jobs they hate and endure humiliation from bosses they don't like, all because they cannot bring themselves to risk their limited security. These suffering people live out their lives in quiet desperation, knowing neither the thrill of victory nor the agony of defeat. They survive by detaching themselves from what they do and fantasize about being in other places doing other things. They become absent when they are present. The joy goes out of their lives, and being with them is no longer fun. It's not that they don't know what's happening. They do. They can sense themselves dying in their jobs, but they haven't got what it takes to launch out into something dangerously new and different.

A man I was counseling told me that although he hated his job, he had twenty-two years invested in his company. He told me that he just couldn't walk out on all the company "benefits" he had accumulated. I responded with dismay and told him that the fact that he had been miserable for the last twenty-two years was not a good enough reason to be unhappy for the next twenty-two years.

Whenever I counsel people whose primary problem in life is tied up with job dissatisfaction, I ask them if they have ever dreamed of doing something different with their lives. In almost every case, these people's faces light up as they describe the glorious plans they have hatched in their minds. But they do not carry out their plans because the plans are full of risks. For a brief time, their eyes flash with excitement and their bodies vibrate with aliveness, but, when I ask them, "Why not do it?" clouds come over their faces and their bodies slump in defeat. Then they give me a hundred and one reasons why they can't. Right before my eyes they repress their dreams because they are afraid to take the risks.

I wonder if these people realize how the deadness of soul that comes from dehumanizing labor affects their mates and their children. I wonder if they grasp the psychic price that they must pay as they live out their lives in apparent absurdity. I wonder if they know that their refusal to take the necessary risks will diminish their energies and render them as lifeless as an uncapped day-old cola drink. I wish I could get them to listen to those older folks who wished they had risked more. In the Bible, we read the fascinating story of the Jews' escape from Egypt and their years of wandering through the wilderness. We read how, when the children of Israel got to the border of "The Promised Land," Moses sent some spies across the Jordan River so that he might learn what his people would face as they went in to possess the land.*

Moses sent in twelve spies. When the twelve returned, they gave varying reports on what they had seen. Ten told of giants who lived in the land and said that challenging them would be foolhardy. These ten spies were afraid to take the risks needed if the children of Israel were to enter the land which God had set aside for them.

On the other hand, there were Joshua and Caleb. These two young men wanted to go for it. They, too, had seen the giants, but they were filled with faith, and they resonated with the challenge that lay before them. These two risk-takers were to become the heroes of God and of Israel. They were the ones who were willing to challenge the odds and live out a dream. They were the ones who were willing to fight unbeatable foes and to live by the impulse to greatness. Joshua and Caleb were risk-takers, and for such risk-takers, there is always a promised land.

* Exod. 14; Num. 13.

It is true that there are great possibilities for failure and, if you fail, there will be those who will mock you. But mockers are not important. Those who like to point when the risk-takers stumble don't count. The criticisms of those who sit back, observe, and offer smug suggestions can be discounted. The Promised Land belongs to the person who takes the risks, whose face is marred with dust and sweat, who strives valiantly while daring everything, who may err and fall, but who has done his or her best. This person's place shall never be with those cold and timid souls who know neither victory nor defeat.

Oh, if only I could persuade timid souls I meet to listen to that inner voice of the Spirit, which challenges us to attempt great things for God and expect great things from God. Oh, if only I could inspire them to heed that inner urging that tells them, "Go for it!" I cannot say what a person should do with life, but I *can* say what a person should *not* do with it. No one should devote one's life to safety, to a course of action that offers no challenge and no fun.

Daring to Go on a Mission for God

I head up a small missionary organization called the Evangelical Association for the Promotion of Education. This organization is committed to work among poor inner city people in Philadelphia and also among the poor in the Dominican Republic and Haiti. The board of directors of EAPE recently interviewed candidates for the position of executive director of overseas operations.

There were many good candidates, any one of whom would have done a good job for us. However, we chose a very young man named Dean Gray. Dean had graduated from Wheaton College and earned a master's degree from Cornell University. He had served as a missionary in the Dominican Republic and had a good grasp of the Spanish language. His qualifications were excellent and his love for Christ was obvious. The other candidates also loved Jesus and were likewise highly qualified, but the board chose Dean primarily because of the way in which he answered one question. The question was "Why do you *want* to do missionary work?" Dean gave the expected responses about wanting to serve others in the name of Christ and wanting to respond to the call of God. Then he ended his answer with the simple statement, "I guess I'll have to admit that one of the main reasons I want to serve Christ on the mission field is because it's fun." That did it. We couldn't help but be attracted to a candidate who could have fun in the midst of all the hardships that would go with the job. We couldn't help but choose a person who would get a kick out of serving others.

I wonder how many of those reading this book have thought about going to the mission field, or maybe considered undertaking some daring work for Christ right here on the home front, but have backed off because of fear of the risks. Perhaps you've been thinking about leaving a job that isn't giving you much fulfillment and doing something heroic for Christ and His Kingdom, but you don't seem to be able to bring yourself to the point where you can "lay aside every weight, and the sin which doth so easily beset [you] and . . . run with patience the race that is set before [you]. . . ."° My advice is to pray long and hard. Get Christian friends to pray with you, and then "go for it."

Sometimes when I suggest such things, people think that I'm laying out a challenge to young people only. Nothing could be farther from the truth. The call to live dangerously for God is for old and young alike. In Genesis 12:4, we read about Abraham, who, when his life was "far spent" (that's the Bible's way of saying that the old man was half dead), left Ur of the Chaldees not knowing where he was going. Can you imagine that 75-year-old man waking one morning and saying to his wife, "Sarah, Sarah, I just had a dream. I just had a vision. God is going to carry out a great mission through us. He is going to create a new nation through us. We are going to be the beginning of a new epoch in human history." Can't you hear his old wife, Sarah, saying, "Go back to bed, Abe. Forget this dreaming stuff. Forget these visions."

"No, Sarah," Abraham must have answered. "Through us God is going to create a new humanity."

"How can this new humanity get started with us, Abe?"

"Glad you asked, Sarah." And then *old* Abe tells her. And both of these old folks fall back into bed laughing.

In the next scene, we see Abraham and Sarah slowly making their way out of Ur of the Chaldees. Their neighbors are yelling after them. . . .

"Where ya goin', Abe?"

° Heb. 12:1.

"Don't know," Abe responds.

"What're ya gonna be doin', Abe?"

"Don't know that either," he calls back.

"Then why are you leavin', Abe?"

"*Because God gave me a vision,*" he declares. "*God gave me a vision.*"

Abraham demonstrated once and for all that you're never too old to respond to the call of God. You're never too old to dream dreams of doing great things for the Kingdom. It's never too late to have visions of significant service. There are mission boards that welcome mature candidates with a lifetime of experience to offer. There are struggling churches that would love to have financially independent pastors, because they lack the resources to pay young seminary graduates. There are Christian organizations all over the world that need senior citizens who are not too old to dream dreams of glorious ways to serve the King of kings.

The Risk-Taking in Friendship

During the course of any given school year at Eastern College, I can count on some freshman coming into my office and complaining about loneliness. I can almost predict that the student will say, "This is supposed to be a Christian college. But if this school is what it's supposed to be, then why am I left so alone? Why isn't anybody paying any attention to me?"

I don't doubt the loneliness of that student. As a matter of fact, I am certain that the student *is* friendless. I am certain that the student *does* suffer from a sense of estrangement. But I also know that the causes of loneliness, friendlessness, and estrangement have nothing to do with the lack of Christianity in the rest of the student body. I know that the student is lonely because he or she is afraid to take the risk of reaching out to others. In the absence of such daring, the paralyzing fear of rejection takes over. Social isolation will always be the lot of those who lack the courage to reach out to others.

Of course, people can reject gestures of Christian affection. We all know that people sometimes rebuff our efforts to be friendly. But, if we do not risk rejection we are inevitably lonely. Jesus can help us to be risk-takers. The good news is that through His strength and help anyone can be courageous enough to take the risks that make friendships possible.

I never tire of telling people that the same Jesus who walked the dusty roads of Palestine two thousand years ago is our resurrected Lord, and He is waiting to be known, loved, and followed here and now. I know this must sound a bit weird to my empirically minded friends, but I must claim, nevertheless, that Jesus is with everyone, every moment of every day. He is invisible, but nevertheless present. He is intangible, but nevertheless waiting to be loved. He does not speak in words that are audible, yet He addresses people in the depths of their being. I am able to declare such incredible truths because I experience them personally whenever I choose to make myself open to Him. I can testify that Jesus is ever waiting and ever available for me and for all who desire His ongoing presence in their lives.

Those of us who live with the awareness of Christ's presence find that He equips us to take the kinds of risks that are necessary to form and sustain strong friendships. Living in a close relationship with Christ convinces us that we are special people. In the words of Scripture, we know the following to be true:

> But as many as received him, to them gave he the power to become the sons of God, even to them that believe on his name . . . (John 1:12).

> For I am persuaded, that neither death, nor life, nor angels, nor principalities, nor powers, nor things present, nor things to come, Nor height, nor depth, nor any other creature, shall be able to separate us from the love of God which is in Christ Jesus our Lord (Rom. 8:38–39).

Those of us who endeavor to live out our lives in the consciousness of this abiding presence know ourselves to be the incredibly precious sons and daughters of God. We know ourselves to be infinitely important to God.

This knowledge gives us a sense of self-worth that makes us able to risk reaching out to others in love. After all, if people reject us they are rejecting the heirs of God. They are rejecting persons whom God has declared to be greater than angels. They are turning their backs on people whom the King of kings has declared His most precious possession. So those of us who have our identities established in God can smile at rejection and say of those who put us down, "You don't know who you're dealing with. . . . You don't know what you're doing."

DOING THINGS THAT LAST

Let's return to the study of the fifty elderly subjects who were asked what they would have done differently if they had life to live over again. "We would have done more things that would live on after we are dead," they said.

There is a latent desire in every human being to do something of worth that will have lasting significance. There is a longing in most people to do something that will make life better for others. According to the Spanish existentialist Miguel de Unamuno, "There is an urge in every man to render himself indispensable."

When we confront the reality of death, we become fully aware of the importance of leaving something good behind. That is why young people give little thought to the significance of their lives, while the elderly think about it all the time. In the face of the end of life, questions about its significance loom large. Many who have been blasé about the meaning of life approach death at the end of it fearing that their epitaph will read like that on the tomb of the poet Keats: "Here lies one whose name is writ in water."

A Lesson from Student Recognition Day

Each year we have a student recognition day at our church. On the Sunday between Christmas and New Year's Day, we ask the young people of our church who are students at colleges and universities to give us reports of how their educational experiences have been going. It is a very special Sunday because ours is a Black Baptist church. The older members of our congregation have not had the educational opportunities that our young people enjoy. Consequently, they love to hear about what their children and grandchildren are learning.

On one such Sunday, after half a dozen students had given their reports, my pastor got up and delivered some closing words. "Children," he said, "you're doing to *die!* You may not think you're going to die. But you're going to die. One of these days, they're going to take you out to the cemetery, drop you in a hole, throw some dirt on your face, and go back to the church and eat potato salad.

"When you were born," he said, "you alone were crying and everybody else was happy. The important question I want to ask is this: When you die are you alone going to be happy, leaving everybody else crying? The answer depends on whether you live to get titles or you live to get testimonies. When they lay you in the grave, are people going to stand around reciting the fancy titles you earned, or are they going to stand around giving testimonies of the good things you did for them? Will they list your degrees and awards, or will they tell about what a blessing you were to them? Will you leave behind just a newspaper column telling people how important you were, or will you leave crying people who give testimonies of how they've lost the best friend they ever had? There's nothing wrong with titles. Titles are good things to have. But if it ever comes down to a choice between a title or a testimony—go for the testimony."

Then he went on a "poetic rip." He went on the kind of rip that makes Black preaching extra special. He went through the Bible talking about those people who had titles and the ones who had testimonies. He rhythmically shouted his sermon, each line stronger than the one before:

> Pharaoh may have had the title . . .
> But Moses had the testimony!
>
> Nebuchadnezzar may have had the title . . .
> But Daniel had the testimony!
>
> Queen Jezebel may have had the title . . .
> But Elijah had the testimony!

He went on and on like that, citing on the one hand Biblical characters who had power and prestige, and on the other, the people of God whose lives were testimonies of loving service. Each line and refrain was greeted with shouts of godly praise from the congregation. The people shouted "Amen!" and "Preach it, pastor!" more loudly and more enthusiastically with each refrain. The upraised hands and the cries of "Well!" gave all the evidence needed that this preacher was "on" and that people were being blessed. He kept it up, hammering away at the contrasts that exist between those who have the titles and those who have the testimonies. When he got to the climax of his message, he simply screamed, **"Pilate may have had the title—"** . . . then he paused for what seemed like an eternity before letting fly . . . **"But my JESUS had the testimony!"**

The old people whose values we are considering would have approved of my pastor's message. They would have agreed that testimonies are more important than titles. They would have agreed that those things we do for others which will be remembered after we are gone are the things that should be our top priority. It is so easy to get our values distorted and to treat the accolades of the media and the write-ups in *Who's Who* as the most significant things in life. But these elderly folks remind us that it is the loving things we do for people that eventually prove to be the most memorable.

My son Bart was an outstanding high school soccer player. He won a lot of trophies and earned the recognition that goes with making all-star teams. He set shutout records as a goalie and carried himself with distinction when he played the game.

When Bart went out for the soccer team during his first year of high school, he had to compete for the goalie position with a senior who, up until Bart's arrival

60

on the scene, seemed assured of the starting position. But Bart beat him out. Bart got the call to start the first game of the season and his competition, this long-time senior player, must have been terribly disappointed. A lesser person might have quit in bitterness at being replaced by a newcomer. A more typical boy might have borne a grudge against the one who took his place on the team. But this boy, whose name was Joel, was very special. He was a Christian and his relationship to Christ was very evident in his behavior. Instead of withdrawing from the team and turning against Bart, Joel became the team's best cheerleader and my son's friend. Joel drove Bart to games, went to parties with him, and, most importantly, asked him to be part of the youth group at his church.

Early one Saturday morning, I heard the horn of Joel's car beeping in our driveway. I looked out of our bedroom window and saw my son scurry out of the house and jump into Joel's car. The two of them were away for several hours and when they got home Bart came directly into my study. He sat down and said, "Dad, I made an important decision this morning. I committed my life to Christ. Joel asked me to turn my life over to Jesus and to become a Christian, and I said I would."

As a Christian father, I had talked to my son on many occasions about Jesus and had asked him many times to surrender his life to Christ. As a preacher, I had taken him to countless evangelistic meetings where he heard me preach the gospel and invite people to make decisions for salvation and for Christian service. But sometimes a boy has barriers against accepting what his father is trying to say; sometimes he finds it easier to receive the gospel from somebody who isn't a part of his family. That was certainly the case with Bart. Joel was able to get through to him in ways that seemed impossible for me. However, I doubt that Joel could have done what he did if he had not backed up his verbal testimony with a living testimony. I doubt that what Joel had to say would have borne any weight with my son if Joel had not demonstrated Christlikeness in the gracious way he treated Bart and reacted to the circumstances that surrounded those soccer tryouts.

By the end of the soccer season, Bart had earned a lot of titles, but Joel had earned a fantastic testimony. And, on that final day when we all stand before the Lord and all that we are and have done is judged, I am sure that Bart's trophies and titles won't mean a thing. But I am also sure that, on that day, my son will be willing and ready to give a testimony about what a difference Joel made in his life.

Given the choice, it's always better to go for a testimony rather than a title. Furthermore, by doing the Christlike thing, Joel saved himself from what might have been a very long and painful school year. He might have been sullen and nasty about his displacement within the soccer team. He might have been a very unhappy person. Instead, he had a great year, made a friend, and experienced some gratifications that are bound to last throughout eternity. Joel found that following Jesus delivered him from bitterness and opened up a relationship that offered him a lot of *fun*.

Fun Is in Little Things

Sometimes people think that the only significant things they do are those for which they receive public recognition. Understandably, we all have a fascination with big-ness and fame. Sometimes we are deluded into thinking that if we could just have the chance to preach to the hundreds of thousands of people that Billy Graham does we would be doing something worthwhile. We think that in order to do something of ultimate importance we must write the great American novel or paint some artistic mas-terpiece. There is a common notion that significance in life depends on some kind of public recognition. But such is not the case. Really gratifying deeds are often done quietly and with hardly any recognition.

One day I was on an airplane traveling from Orlando, Florida, to Philadelphia. I was settled down in a window seat when I happened to glance across the aisle to the other side of the plane. There, seated next to the window opposite mine, was one of the most sophisticated and attractive women I have ever seen. She was absolutely stunning. It was hard to take my eyes off her.

After a few minutes, a very macho-looking, "with-it" guy got on the plane. He was almost a stereotype of the kind of guy who hangs out at singles bars. His satin shirt was unbuttoned down to his waist so that he could pub-licly let the "chicks" see the curls of hair on his chest and the gaudy gold chains hanging around his neck. With great interest, I watched as he "moved" down the aisle of the plane. He spotted the empty seat next to the stunning woman who had been holding my attention. He sat down next to her and then he "did his thing." He made moves that a New York "make-out man" would have admired. And in no time at all he had the young woman thoroughly involved in conversation, hanging on his every word. As a sociologist, I was fascinated with this interactive process. But then an unexpected and exciting thing happened. When he had her completely engaged, she made *her* move and pulled a reversal, suddenly extracting a Bible from her shoulder bag. Before the guy could figure out was was happening, she was laying the gospel on him. Her eyes sparkling with excitement, she began telling him all about Jesus. She pointed out verse after verse that showed the way of salvation. I must admit that this sudden turn of events amused me. At one point, I had to bite my tongue to keep from laughing. But this was no laughing matter. Brilliantly and seriously, she told the story of God's salvation, and after his initial shock, he began to listen to her with genuine interest.

The plane landed in Philadelphia on schedule and rolled up to the reception gate so that the passengers could disembark. Everyone squeezed into the aisle and stood in the usual convoluted fashion, waiting for the people up front to get off. It was as I was standing in the aisle that I noticed that the "make-out man" and the gorgeous woman were not standing. Instead, they were both seated with their heads bowed in prayer. She had her hand on his shoulder and I knew that, with that prayer, he was accepting Christ as his Savior and Lord.

That woman will not be granted an honorary doctorate for what she did. No magazine will nominate her as "Woman of the Year." No mention will be made in the evening news of what she did that day, but it will have eternal significance. She did something that will live on long after she is dead.

Doing Things in Secret

Sometimes, the most important things that are done are done anonymously. For instance, I know of a man who loves to use his money to provide help for people who will never know who he is. On one occasion, I told him about a student of mine at Eastern College who was hoping to be a minister but was going to have to drop out of school because of his lack of funds. This man contacted the college treasurer and arranged to have the bills paid. That student became one of the best preachers in my denomination. Hundreds of people have become Christians under his leadership. Thousands of lives have been influenced by his sermons. And he never did find out who put up the money to keep him in school, but he often reminds me to tell that man of his gratitude. Behind it all, there was a person with resources and the desire to do something that would live on after he was dead.

What surprises me is that more people don't do this sort of thing. So many people keep their money carefully tucked away, and when they die, they often leave it to people who don't really need it. What a wasted opportunity to do things that would live on. They could make a major difference in many lives. Like the man I just described, they could sponsor candidates for the ministry or the mission field. Every year, young people who are desperately needed in mission service drop out of school when a gift of a few thousand dollars could have kept them on track towards a church vocation. People with some extra money could have done things which might have had eternal significance for these missionary candidates.

It seems tragic to me that thousands of young people work diligently to get through college or seminary, but never fulfill their mission field calling and dream because they graduate deeply in debt. They know that if they go to the mission field, they won't be able to earn the kind of money that will enable them to pay what they owe. They delay going to the field, and before they realize what is happening, they are married, have children and are more deeply in debt than ever before. Peter Wagner, one of the prime leaders of the Church Growth movement, claims that we lose three-quarters of our missionary candidates this way. This immeasurable loss could be avoided if only people who had some extra money would help them.

Some people have contacted me to offer such financial support. In most cases, years after I have arranged for them to help ministerial students or missionary candidates, I get letters telling me about the *fun* they have had watching the ministries of the young men and women whose service they made possible. Many times, I have arranged support for the training of students who come to study with me from Third World nations. When these students graduate and return to their homelands to serve their native churches, their benefactors have the *fun* of visiting the work that is being done and of seeing the blessings their gifts made possible. To tell the truth, I can't think of anything people could do with their money that would give them more pleasure.

You may ask me how you can have testimonies given on your behalf if the people who are blessed by what you do don't even know who blessed them. The answer to that question is glorious. It comes from Jesus himself, who told us, ". . . and thy Father which seeth in secret himself shall reward thee openly."*

Won't it be *fun* on Judgment Day when Jesus tells the person you helped anonymously that it was you who was such a blessing? Won't it be fun when that person responds with happy surprise and screams, "So you're the one? You sly one, you. I never even guessed that it might be you." Surprise parties are always the best kind, and those who give and bless in secret are headed for the biggest surprise party of them all.

I know one person who needed a job desperately and couldn't get one. I pulled some strings and made some phone calls. I arranged for him to get a job that he could have never gotten on his own. That job changed his life and saved his marriage. He knows that somebody worked hard on his behalf, but he doesn't know who it was. I can hardly wait to see his face when Jesus tells him that it was I. I'm going to have some real *fun* on that day.

Glory in the Undramatic

Some of the most important things we do in life are often neither dramatic nor memorable. Happily, on Judgment Day, Jesus will reward a lot of people who hardly remember the important things for which they will be honored.† Sending a card of appreciation to someone who is a bit down and needs a lift, visiting a shut-in who is lonely, baby-sitting for a harried mother who needs a

---

* Matt. 6:4b.
† Matt. 25:39, 44.

few hours off, calling someone on the phone to show that you care, and giving a glass of cool water in the name of Christ are not the sorts of things that we even remember doing after they are done. But the people we do them for often remember, and I know that Jesus never forgets.

Being Nice

A little girl once prayed, "God, make all the bad people good and all the good people nice." Too often the good people in the church aren't very nice people. They do not understand how important niceness is.

One of my wife's favorite sayings is "It's nice to be important, but it's more important to be nice." The people we think are great Christians because they are doing things that society thinks are important may not be quite as significant in the Kingdom of God as those who have been faithful in doing little things for others. My wife certainly belongs to that legion of nice people God will invite to enter His Kingdom and sit on His Right Hand. My two children agree with me that she is one of the nicest people in the world. She spends most of her time figuring out little things she can do for people to make them feel better. When I try to praise her for what she does, she simply says, "It's no big deal. What I do makes me happy." She visits the elderly each week, sends thoughtful notes to people, and offers friendship to many people who have no friends. These are the things that will live on after she is gone. To her, Jesus will one day say, "Thou hast been faithful over a few things, I will make thee ruler over many things: enter thou into the joy of thy lord."°

The Special Story of Miss Thompson

I know of a schoolteacher named Miss Thompson. Every year, when she met her new students, she would say, "Boys and girls, I love you all the same. I have no favorites." Of course, she wasn't being completely truthful. Teachers do have favorites and, what is worse, most teachers have students that they just don't like.

Teddy Stallard was a boy that Miss Thompson just didn't like, and for good reason. He just didn't seem interested in school. There was a dead-pan, blank expression on his face and his eyes had a glassy, unfocused appearance. When she spoke to Teddy, he always answered in monosyllables. His clothes were musty and his hair was unkempt. He wasn't an attractive boy and he certainly wasn't likable.

Whenever she marked Teddy's papers, she got a certain perverse pleasure out of putting X's next to the wrong answers and when she put the F's at the top of the papers, she always did it with a flair. She should have known better; she had Teddy's records and she knew more about him than she wanted to admit. The records read:

1st Grade: Teddy shows promise with his work and attitude, but poor home situation.

° Matt. 25:21.

2nd Grade: Teddy could do better. Mother is seriously ill. He receives little help at home.

3rd Grade: Teddy is a good boy, but too serious. He is a slow learner. His mother died this year.

4th Grade: Teddy is very slow, but well-behaved. His father shows no interest.

Christmas came and the boys and girls in Miss Thompson's class brought her Christmas presents. They piled their presents on her desk and crowded around to watch her open them. Among the presents, there was one from Teddy Stallard. She was surprised that he had brought her a gift, but he had. Teddy's gift was wrapped in brown paper and was held together with Scotch tape. On the paper were written the simple words, "For Miss Thompson from Teddy." When she opened Teddy's present, out fell a gaudy rhinestone bracelet, with half the stones missing, and a bottle of cheap perfume.

The other boys and girls began to giggle and smirk over Teddy's gifts, but Miss Thompson at least had enough sense to silence them by immediately putting on the bracelet and putting some of the perfume on her wrist. Holding her wrist up for the other children to smell, she said, "Doesn't it smell lovely?" And the children, taking their cue from the teacher, readily agreed with "oo's" and "ah's."

At the end of the day, when school was over and the other children had left, Teddy lingered behind. He slowly came over to her desk and said softly, "Miss Thompson . . . Miss Thompson, you smell just like my mother . . . and her bracelet looks real pretty on you too. I'm glad you liked my presents."

When Teddy left, Miss Thompson got down on her knees and asked God to forgive her.

The next day when the children came to school, they were welcomed by a new teacher. Miss Thompson had become a different person. She was no longer just a teacher; she had become an agent of God. She was now a person committed to loving her children and doing things for them that would live on after her. She helped all the children, but especially the slow ones, and especially Teddy Stallard. By the end of that school year, Teddy showed dramatic improvement. He had caught up with most of the students and was even ahead of some.

She didn't hear from Teddy for a long time. Then one day, she received a note that read:

Dear Miss Thompson:

I wanted you to be the first to know. I will be graduating second in my class.

Love,

Teddy Stallard

Four years later, another note came:

Dear Miss Thompson:

They just told me I will be graduating first in my class. I wanted you to be the first to know. The university has not been easy, but I liked it.

Love,

Teddy Stallard

And, four years later:

Dear Miss Thompson:

As of today, I am Theodore Stallard, M.D. How about that?
I wanted you to be the first to know. I am getting married
next month, the 27th to be exact. I want you to come and sit
where my mother would sit if she were alive. You are the
only family I have now; Dad died last year.

Love,

Teddy Stallard

Miss Thompson went to that wedding and sat where
Teddy's mother would have sat. She deserved to sit there;
she had done something for Teddy that he could never
forget.

Miss Thompson and Barnabas

In many ways, Miss Thompson is comparable to Barnabas. Barnabas never wrote an epistle. We find no evidence that there was a major church founded by him.
Yet in Acts 11:24 we are told that Barnabas "was a good
man, and full of the Holy Ghost and of faith; and [many]
people were added unto the Lord." He was a man who
may not have earned a lot of titles, but he certainly
earned a pile of testimonies.

We meet Barnabas three times in the Book of Acts.*
The first time we encounter him, he is selling his land so
he can have money for some of his poor brothers and sisters in the church. The second time is when the Apostle
Paul is trying to gain acceptance by a church that is suspi-
cious of him because of his reputation as a persecutor of

* Acts 4:36–37; 9:27; 15:37.

72

Christians. Barnabas vouches for Paul and introduces him to the other Christians as a brother in the Lord.

The third time we meet Barnabas, he is standing up for John Mark, who is being rejected by Paul. John Mark had gone with Paul and Barnabas on their first missionary journey. When things had become difficult and persecution had become too much for him to handle, John Mark left Paul and Barnabas and returned home. Later, when Paul and Barnabas returned home themselves, a repentant John Mark begged for a second chance, but Paul was reluctant to give John Mark his trust again. Yet Paul was the one who wrote in Galatians 6:1: "Brethren, if a man be overtaken in a fault, ye which are spiritual, restore such an one in the spirit of meekness; considering thyself, lest thou also be tempted."

Barnabas knew how to live out those words. It was Barnabas who took John Mark with him and gave him another chance for missionary service. If Barnabas had not been more forgiving than Paul, who rejected John Mark and took Silas as his missionary partner, we might not have the Gospel of Mark.

Barnabas never did the kind of big time stuff that would have made him the biblical standout that Paul became. He was committed to doing what might at first seem like little things for Christ and the Church. On the other hand, the precious kindnesses of Barnabas would be remembered by those who survived him. If I had a choice of hanging out with either Paul or Barnabas, I would choose Barnabas. I am sure that a nice guy like Barnabas, who was constantly earning testimonies by doing little things, must have been more fun to be with over the long haul.

Part Two

ON THE JOB

I OWE, I OWE, IT'S OFF TO WORK WE GO

came of age during the 1950s. Consequently, and like many of my generation, I was taught to believe in the Protestant work ethic. Those principles encouraged me to look upon work as a virtue and laziness as a sin. I was taught the "poor Richard" sayings of Benjamin Franklin, sayings such as:

- Idle hands are the devil's workshop.
- A stitch in time saves nine.
- A rolling stone gathers no moss.
- A penny saved is a penny earned.
- A fool and his money are soon parted.

These simple instructions were part of a moral system that made productivity a godly mandate and the accumulation of wealth the test of true virtue.

Max Weber, one of the founding fathers of modern sociology, traced the origins of this work ethic. His research and study of economic behavior among the people of Europe led him to conclude that there was something about Protestantism that encouraged hard work and thrift. He noticed that in those countries where Protestantism dominated, people seemed to be more industrious, more thrifty, and consequently, more affluent than predominately Catholic countries. Anyone traveling across Europe who carefully observes the economic activities of the people notices the same thing.

I remember taking a European tour with my family and finding out for myself how the religious ethos of respective nations influenced what they did and how they did it. In Switzerland, the home of the Protestant reformers Calvin and Zwingli, there was an atmosphere of intensity. Everyone I saw seemed to be busy doing something important. Everyone was working, and everything was functioning with precision. Nothing seemed to be broken in Switzerland. All the lawns were neatly trimmed, no trash was to be found on the sides of roads, and the whole countryside appeared to have been recently manicured by a flock of angels. Zurich was particularly interesting to me. Hard-working capitalists were everywhere evident. I enjoyed sitting in the train station in Zurich and checking the movement of the trains in respect to the schedule. When the Swiss railroad claimed that a train was to leave at a particular time, I could count on it leaving precisely at the designated hour.

After a brief stay in Zurich, my family and I boarded a train bound for Rome. The trip over the Alps provided breathtaking vistas, and the Swiss train traveled according to a precise plan. All went well until we got to Milan, Italy. After arriving in the station, our train sat still for almost three hours. There was supposed to be an engine change in Milan with the Italians providing the new locomotive that would take us on to Rome. But my Italian compadres could not find an available engine, and furthermore, none of them seemed to care. When I asked a conductor what was happening, he shrugged his shoulders, smiled, and said, "Who knows?" He might as well have said, "Who cares?"—because nobody did—nobody, that is, except us Americans. The Italian businessmen who were on the train took it all in good-humored fashion. One man pulled an accordion out of nowhere. Another produced a bottle of wine and some sandwiches. People began singing. And, before I realized what was happening, I found myself in the midst of a party. Their easy-going, leisurely attitudes were quite a contrast to what I had just left behind in Switzerland.

Most young people who are reared in a strict Calvinistic setting can attest to what I am saying. Imagine a traditional, old-line Presbyterian businessman getting ready for a vacation. Can't you hear him as he gives his last set of instructions to his family? "Tomorrow, we leave on a vacation. We're going to leave at six in the morning." To the groans of the rest of the family, he quickly responds, "I want to get an early start and not waste time. When you get into that car," he continues, "the gas tank will be full and your bladders will be empty. We will drive and drive until the gasoline tank is empty and your bladders will then be allowed to be full. And may the Lord have mercy upon you if your bladders should become full before that gas tank is empty."

The contrast between the work ethic of Protestants and the more relaxed attitude toward work among Catholics is evident even in our hemisphere. The population of the United States, which up until the last few decades was dominated by a Protestant ethos, reflects an attitude toward work that is different from that in Latin America. Even Catholics in the United States, according to sociologist Gerhard Lanski, act in accord with the work orientation of Protestantism.

The Diligent Calvinists

Of all the Protestants, the Calvinists have been the most diligent workers. Methodists and Lutherans certainly have been more intense about work and the accumulation of wealth than their Catholic brothers and sisters, but none of them have been able to match the Calvinists' commitment. I think it is no accident that the center of capitalism is Geneva, the same city where John Calvin led his movement for religious reform.

Weber believed the origins of this diligence could be traced to Calvinistic theology. There were four elements in the Calvinistic belief system that represented hard work as a virtue and thereby generated a religious motivation for the accumulation of wealth. These four doctrines are:

I Owe, I Owe, It's Off to Work We Go

1. The doctrine of predestination.
2. The belief that wealth is evidence of divine election.
3. The doctrine of a calling.
4. The doctrine of thrift.

The Calvinists believe that those who are to be saved and enjoy eternal life have been "chosen" for this salvation before the foundation of the world. Of course, the flip side of that doctrine promoted the idea that those who are doomed to hell likewise have been predestined to their eternal state of being. (There are theologians who argue that this emphasis on "double" predestination by the Calvinists was more extreme than what Calvin himself taught.)

Such theological positions left people with a very serious question: how can we know who is among the elect and who is not? Or, stated another way: how can a person know if his/her destiny is salvation or condemnation? The response that Calvinists gave to this question is one that many find offensive and others find anti-Christian. Boldly stated, the answer is as follows: those who are predestined for salvation will know that they are among the elect by virtue of the fact that they prosper economically. (It should be noted that this was a doctrine of Calvinists and not necessarily a doctrine promoted by Calvin himself.) Quite simply, this means that people who are saved, and hence true Christians, are assured of their spiritual state because they become rich. Conversely, those who are not in tune with the will of God and are spiritually lost are more likely to suffer from poverty and bad fortune.

There is some Biblical support for this belief system, particularly in the Old Testament. From the history of the Jews, we learn that when Israel was in a right relationship with God, its people prospered, and when it was estranged from God and disobedient to His will, the people suffered socially and economically. The Jews believed that not being godly might mean that they would experience famine and conquest by their enemies. Furthermore, the prosperity of the patriarchs of the Old Testament, including that of such men as Abraham, Isaac, and Jacob, gives evidence that a right relationship with God results in wealth and well-being.

Modern Consequences of Prosperity Theology

The belief that the saved prosper has had painful effects on the psyche of contemporary poor people. In Protestant nations such as the United States, it is more than inconvenient to be poor, it is downright unspiritual. The poor in the slums and on the tenant farms of the United States seem overwhelmed with sadness and despair. In contrast, anyone who travels to Latin America and visits the slums and barrios is taken aback by the fact that the poor in those Catholic nations seem to have a contagious joy and happiness about them. According to the followers of sociologist Max Weber, this is due to the different interpretations attached to poverty by each of these groups of poor people. In Latin America, poverty does not have the negative spiritual connotations that it does in the United States. In Latin America, people believe that Jesus regards the poor as deserving of the special blessing of God,* whereas the Protestant ethos of the

* Luke 6:20.

United States leads us to the view that the rich are the blessed of God and the poor persons are alienated from Him.

This Calvinistic value system is alive and well in modern America, particularly under the auspices of the "electronic church." One after another, television evangelists promise us that faithfulness to God brings wealth and health. In program after program, the message that comes across is that if the viewers and hearers become Christians and do the will of God (which sometimes includes sending a financial contribution to the evangelist), they can expect to get high-paying jobs and to enjoy a long and healthy life.

I have trouble with this kind of message. I suppose my negative reaction stems from my experiences on the mission field. In places throughout Latin America and Africa, I have come to know many people who love Christ in ways that make my love for Him pale by comparison. Nevertheless, they suffer from grinding poverty. I guess my negative feelings come from having seen too many instances where the wicked prosper while the righteous are oppressed, as mentioned in Psalms 73:12.

What particularly bothers me is that this kind of theology has become the justification for some Christians to reject the pleas to provide economic and social assistance for people in poor countries. Time and time again, when I have pleaded with my affluent Christian brothers and sisters to participate in supporting church-sponsored job training programs, feeding programs for children, schools, hospitals and other social projects, I have encountered opposition.

The Christians who question such efforts contend that

all such help to the poor of the world is valueless and will come to nothing. They argue that until people come to know Christ, they will never prosper economically, and until they know Christ, all efforts to improve social conditions are a waste of time. They believe that all we have to do is to preach the gospel and save souls and socioeconomic development will take care of itself.

While I usually find their attitude abominably selfish, I cannot completely discount what they say. There is some truth to the idea that Christian conversion influences economic activity. People who are deeply committed Christians do tend to translate their faith into creative economic productivity. Converts to Christ usually *can* be counted on to evidence changes in their lifestyle that foster economic prosperity.

Several years ago, while touring a Latin American country, I came upon a mountain village which in many ways demonstrated the worst that can happen to a demoralized, economically oppressed community in a Third World nation. Unemployment was rampant; family life was threatened by the infidelity of men trying to prove their manhood; alcoholism was an omnipresent problem; and dishonesty was a way of life.

Several years later, I happened upon the same village. During this second visit, I was amazed at the changes evident everywhere. While the community by no means had become an approximation of Calvin's Geneva, it was markedly different. There was an industrious spirit among people. Some of them had organized a coffee cooperative and coffee growers were earning almost twice as much as before. The streets of the village were clean and, while the local cantina was still doing a thriving business, it was no longer the center of village life. The dilapidated local school had been fixed up and painted, and there was a completely different atmosphere in the village.

When I asked about the changes, a local fundamentalist missionary told me in a disgruntled way that the changes were largely the result of the leadership of the Catholic priest. "He got mixed up with some Pentecostals down in the capital city," the missionary explained. "When he came back to the village, he started to talk to people about the 'Second Blessing' and being filled with the Holy Spirit. It wasn't long before he had half this town speaking in tongues."

I asked what was wrong with all of that. Had there been negative consequences that followed this Pentecostal revival?

"Oh," responded the missionary, "there were improvements in the way people lived. A lot of people turned from immorality and became industrious. But don't you see—that's the way Satan works. He's got these people so far into the charismatic movement that they think they are experiencing true Christianity!"

No, I did not see! I am not one to speak in tongues or to manifest some of the more spectacular charismatic gifts like healing, but it was impossible for me to see the changes that had taken place in that community as anything else but the work of God. How could that missionary think that Satan would cast out Satan?° How could this otherwise godly man be so entrenched in his theological presuppositions that the obvious outpouring and work of God were not clear to him?

° Matt. 12:26.

I cite this experience not to put down my missionary friend. In his own way, he was making a very significant contribution for Christ in that village. Rather, my reason for citing his story is to give evidence that Christian conversion can have economic consequences even if we don't want to acknowledge the possibility. However, I simultaneously want to affirm that it is a mistake to establish too simple a relationship between Christian conversion and economic prosperity. In many places in the world, people who are converted and adopt Biblically prescribed lifestyles will languish in desperate privation because of the prevailing society's structural evil. In some places in the world, the political system prevents economic progress, even among devout followers of Christ. In South Africa, for instance, racist policies prevent some of the saints from ever achieving very much. In other places, the economic domination of the local economy by huge multinational corporations based in other nations hinders the prosperity of indigenous peoples.

But when all other things are equal, the value system engendered by conversions to Christ does enhance economic well-being. However, all other things are seldom equal. That is why Christians should be committed to destroying apartheid in South Africa, to ending the domination of Poland by Russia, and to abolishing dictatorships in such countries as Chile. Wherever there are political economic arrangements which reduce people to poverty by no fault of their own, Christians must act to change those arrangements. Because, when there is a just socioeconomic order, *then* Christian conversion will foster those traits that make for economic prosperity.

I Owe, I Owe, It's Off to Work We Go

The Doctrine of "A Calling"

Max Weber recognized that Protestantism promoted a new attitude toward Christian vocation. The Catholicism of the Middle Ages urged people who wanted to serve God with the totality of their being to leave their worldly vocations and go to convents and monasteries. In contrast, the Reformers (and particularly Calvin) argued that Christians need not be separated from the business of worldly economic activities in order to render Christian service. The Protestant reformers proposed that Christ could be served with total commitment in ordinary vocations. Bakers, carpenters, farmers, and artisans all could serve God in their respective activities if they were able to view their work as a primary way of serving God. Ordinary economic production could be godly, they argued, if the products were a testimony to the faith of the producers. The Calvinists believed that dedicated Christians could be counted on to work diligently at all times, not just when their employers were watching, because of such scriptures as Matthew 24:14. The products of Christians, they taught, should never evidence a slipshod quality, because these superior products were supposed to glorify the God who motivated their producers. Every worker, regardless of how humble his task, was to view work as a religious discipline.

Recently I made a trip to Scotland. Since my work took me to Glasgow, I was able to visit a small shipbuilding community located near that city. This town was the birthplace of my father-in-law, and my wife, who was traveling with me, was most eager to see the place where her family had its roots.

Upon arriving, Peggy had a strange and almost mystical feeling that this was a place where she could belong. She felt a sense of "at-homeness" immediately. We talked to a few people on the streets of the town and then asked a middle-aged woman for directions to the local shipyard because we wanted to visit the place where Peggy's grandfather had worked. The woman was pleased to tell us that she was at that very moment on her way to her job on the evening shift at the shipyard and would be glad to take us there personally.

On our way we passed numerous shipbuilders who had just finished their work on the daytime shift. Each of them bid an enthusiastic greeting to our new friend. Everybody we passed knew her by name and she, likewise, knew everyone we encountered. There was a fun-loving quality about her personality, and her whole demeanor communicated that she was enjoying life.

"What's your job at the shipyard?" I asked. She stopped in her tracks, took my arm, and then spoke to me in such a way that I was sure she was about to tell me something of enormous importance.

"What do *I* do?" she asked rhetorically. "What do *I* do?" she asked a second time, as if I had not caught the question the first time. "I'm the one who cleans the ships." And then, obviously impressed with the importance of her task, she added, "And you know, nary a ship goes to sea until I say it's clean enough. It's my job to see to it that every bit of dirt is polished away. That's what I do."

I was duly impressed. She was a woman who saw dignity in her labor. Raised in the Calvinistic tradition of the Scottish reformer, John Knox, she was proud of what she did because she viewed her work as a holy calling. It was this attitude toward work that infused the people who built America. It was this enthusiasm that made American craftsmanship the best in the world.

I can remember when the label "Made in Japan" meant that a product was inferior, and when American-made cars were the most carefully crafted automobiles in the world. There was a time when the Protestant work ethic created an attitude toward work that caused even the most common of industrial tasks to be undertaken with pride. If the Protestant work ethic has begun to die in America, we all will be losers.

The Doctrines of Thrift

Christians infused with the Protestant work ethic labor diligently. They feel guilty about laziness. They glorify God through their work. Their godly attitude toward their labor makes them productive, and the more productive they are, the more they prosper. However, there are some important admonitions about money which the old-time Protestant preachers carefully communicated to their congregations: "Be careful not to waste your money," they said. "All wealth belongs to God and should be spent only in accord with His will. Thrift is a very important virtue and should be evident in the lives of all Christians."

I was taught these views as I grew up. Over and over again I was told to heed the message of "The Parable of the Talents" that Jesus told in verses 14–30 of Matthew 25. Just as the three servants were entrusted with caring for their master's money to the best of their ability, I was told I should do the best I can with what I've been given. If I were like the servants who were given five talents and two talents (a "talent" was an amount of money in biblical days), and I put my talents to work in order to make something with them, then I would be rewarded. But if I were like the one-talent servant who was afraid and did nothing with what was entrusted to him, then what I had would be taken away. The meaning was made very clear to me then. And don't think the last part of the parable about that unprofitable servant being thrown into the outer darkness with all that weeping and gnashing of teeth was lost on this little kid!

It was okay for Christians to make money, according to the Protestant preachers, but it was not good to spend it. Money, they believed, should be saved and *invested*. Economic resources should be used to gain more wealth.

Such values have caused Protestants, particularly Calvinists, to become rather somber people who look with suspicion upon those who spend money on pleasure. Their plain and sober approach to living stands in sharp contrast to the traditions of my Catholic Italian relatives. Consequently, it's more fun to be in Rome than in Geneva!

Once I was invited to speak at a church in Las Vegas, Nevada, the gambling capital of America. I was met at the airport by a solid Calvinist preacher who, on the way to the hotel where I was staying, proceeded to lecture me on the evils of gambling. From his Calvinistic perspective, he viewed gambling as an inappropriate way of using money that belonged to God. "It's wrong to gamble with somebody else's money," he said to me, "and all money belongs to God."

I had no basis upon which to disagree with him. If Jesus Christ is "Lord of all," then all things belong to Him. Indeed, to gamble is to use resources that belong to God in a way that is contrary to His will. Certainly, when we consider the needs of the hungry in Third World countries, the need for funds to undergird the missionary enterprise, and the financial needs that exist in local churches, we have to believe that wasting money in slot machines and at gambling tables is wrong. According to the Protestant work ethic, wealth should be earned by rendering diligent service to others in the name of Christ. It should not come by chance and without honest labor.

What seemed a bit strange to me was that this pastor took me to the MGM Hotel, the primary gambling center of the city, explaining that it was good stewardship for me to stay there. He pointed out that by offering people low room rates the hotel tries to lure them to stay there and gamble. Since I did not gamble, I could stay at this luxurious hotel at a very low cost and, I suppose, have more money to give to missionaries. At the time, it all seemed to make sense to me.

The next morning, the pastor planned to pick me up at the hotel and take me to preach at his church, but the appointed hour passed and he did not show up. As I stood waiting, looking through the glass doors of the hotel, I had my hands in my pockets. In my right pocket there was a single tempting quarter. "Who goes to Las Vegas," I thought, "and doesn't throw one lousy quarter in a slot machine? Putting one quarter into a one-armed bandit won't make me a gambler. It will be fun to pull the magic handle and hope for some good fortune." All around me, people were gambling, throwing dice and trying their luck at slots. No one noticed as I walked over to the nearest machine and deposited my solitary quarter.

Much to my surprise, I hit the jackpot! Quarters came pouring out of that slot machine, making incredibly loud clanging sounds. An alarm bell on top of the machine started ringing like a fire alarm and a strobe light started flashing wildly. I grabbed whole handfuls of quarters and began to stuff them into my pockets. As I was joyfully gathering my newly acquired wealth, I happened to glance out the glass doors of the hotel—and that preacher was coming at me. I asked, "Dear Lord, why are you doing this to me?" Moving quickly, I was able to get every last quarter of my winnings into my pockets as that preacher came through the doors. Then I realized what forty dollars in quarters does to a jacket. I spent the rest of the morning with my hands in my jacket pockets trying to keep them from sagging too much.

Gambling is not on the list of acceptable activities for Protestants and, in spite of my one deviation, I agree that it is wrong. And Protestant work ethic or no, gambling *is* an inappropriate use of God's resources. In reality, it can be a sickness, an addictive practice that has ruined lives and often requires serious psychotherapy to overcome.

The crazy thing is that the Protestant work ethic can "work." It creates what economists call "the wealth-generating cycle." If people work diligently at their jobs because they believe their work to be a calling from God, they probably *will* make money. If they do not squander that money but are religiously motivated to invest it, they probably will make *more* money. The more money they make, the more they are convinced that they are God's elect. The assurance that they are God's elect stimulates gratitude to God for His great salvation. And the primary way to show gratitude to God is through hard work. Thus, the whole process for making and accumulating wealth is cyclical.

Getting Back to the Old Ways

After enduring two decades of criticism from the youth counterculture, the financial value system of the Protestant establishment is gaining support, particularly among young upwardly mobile professionals. The yuppies of the '80s, like their grandparents, see nothing wrong with making a lot of money. They are willing to work hard to do so. However, their penchant for hard work and their appreciation of wealth does not come from deep-rooted religious convictions. It emerges from an egoistic, materialistic philosophy that defines "the good life" as something that rich people can buy. Yuppies want to make a lot of money, not for the benefits that come from believing that wealth is a sign of divine election. Theirs is a worldly attitude that leads them to want to buy the things that seem to make life worthwhile.

One yuppie asked me recently if I thought buying a BMW was a sin. I did not quite know how to answer him. I must admit that having a dependable automobile is a legitimate aspiration for any person living in a modern society characterized by urban sprawl. However, there does seem to be something unchristian about spending

$40,000 on a sports car. I always have to ask myself what kind of car Jesus would buy if He were presently among us in the flesh. Would the Lord spend $40,000 for a BMW? I doubt it. In the face of the desperate hunger and poverty that exists in the world today, I think that Jesus would live more simply in order to use His resources to help those who are simply trying to live.

I believe that Jesus seriously questions a lifestyle of affluence in the presence of poverty. His parable about the rich man and Lazarus (Luke 16:19–31) tells us volumes about His way of thinking. The rich man, dressed in his fine clothing, ate at a sumptuous table. And Lazarus, a beggar covered with sores, lay waiting every day at the rich man's gate in case he might receive a few crumbs that had fallen from the rich man's table. This pattern continued until one day, as Jesus told it, Lazarus and the rich man both died. Lazarus was taken to the "bosom of Abraham," but the rich man went straight to hell. And the rich man begged, then, for Abraham to allow Lazarus to come give him just a drop of water, but Abraham didn't send him. So he begged that Abraham send Lazarus to warn his brothers what would happen when they died if they didn't change their ways. And, of course, Abraham declined again, knowing it wouldn't work. It's an interesting story. The rich man, at least, was worried about his brothers. Really, he may not have been all that bad, in the way we view "badness." His sin was not that he broke any of the Ten Commandments. He wasn't an adulterer or a thief. He hadn't killed anyone and in all probability, he came by his money through hard work. The sin of the rich man was that he enjoyed a yuppie-like "good life" while being unconcerned about those around him who desperately needed help.

Jesus talked about this problem many times. When Jesus encountered the Rich Young Ruler in Mark 10, He had some hard talk that is applicable to the rich young rulers of our day:

> And when he was gone forth into the way, there came one running, and kneeled to him, and asked him, "Good Master, what shall I do that I may inherit eternal life?" And Jesus said unto him, "Why callest thou me good? There is none good but one, that is, God. Thou knowest the commandments, Do not commit adultery, Do not kill, Do not steal, Do not bear false witness, Defraud not, Honour thy father and mother." Then he answered and said unto him, "Master, all these have I observed from my youth." Then Jesus beholding him loved him, and said unto him, "One thing thou lackest: go thy way, sell whatsoever thou hast, and give to the poor, and thou shalt have treasure in heaven: and come, take up the cross, and follow me." And he was sad at that saying, and went away grieved: for he had great possessions (vv. 17–22).

When Jesus challenged the way of life of this young man, He raised some serious questions for disciples in His day and in ours. They, like us, wanted to know if it is ever permissible for followers of Christ to be wealthy. Jesus' answer gives little comfort either to those of us reared on the Protestant work ethic of the past or its modern version espoused by contemporary yuppies: "It is easier for a camel to go through the eye of a needle, than for a rich man to enter into the kingdom of God."* When their

* Mark 10:25.

Master laid this teaching on His followers, they were incredulous. The accumulation of wealth made their religion suspect so far as Jesus was concerned. He told them in Matthew 8 that "foxes have holes and birds of the air have nests; but the Son of man hath not where to lay his head."

The Apostle Paul also reminds us in 2 Corinthians 8:9 that being a Christian means imitating one who was rich, but who for our sakes became poor. Within the worldview of all the New Testament writers, it is clear that the elect of God are not the rich. Instead those who have so responded to the needs of others that they themselves have become poor as it says in Luke 6:24 or 30—they are the truly rich.

Once, when visiting our mission work in Haiti, I had my son with me. As we walked down the streets of Port-au-Prince, we were approached continually by begging children. I warned my son against giving them any money. I said, "Bart, if you start giving away some of your money to these kids, they'll besiege you and not let you go until they've got every penny you own." Bart simply glanced at me with an inquisitive look and answered, "So???"

What a good answer. Isn't that just how a Christian should answer when confronted with such a warning? The Apostle John clearly states that if a rich person knows of someone in need, but does not respond to that need, then his talk about possessing the love of God is hypocritical.°

° 1 John 3:17–18.

The Difficult Task of Giving

The Protestant work ethic prevents us from being an easy touch. Those who are reared in this tradition of hard work have some serious questions about just giving money away. They fear that the wrong kind of charity can be extremely destructive. Certainly Charles Murray, in his controversial book *Losing Ground*, gives much validation to the claim that the good-hearted giving of money to poor people without proper accountability can destroy personal initiative and create dehumanizing dependency.

In ancient Hebraic literature there are some significant guidelines for giving to the poor. On a graded basis, the highest form of charity is creating jobs for the poor while keeping them from knowing what you have done for them. Of less virtue is creating jobs that are not necessary jobs, jobs the recipients know have been created for them. This is like my calling my Uncle Tom and telling him that my daughter needs a summer job at his auto repair shop. If he tells me that there are no openings but to send her down anyway and he'll find something for her to do, this isn't an ideal arrangement, but it certainly beats a handout.

The third way to help the poor is to send them money anonymously. That way the recipients do not feel embarrassed when they encounter the giver.

The least desirable form of charity is to give money to the poor when they are fully aware of who the givers are. Such giving humiliates the poor and may even engender bitterness.

Every Christmas, church youth groups decide that their members can demonstrate the Christmas spirit by making up food baskets for poor families in their communities. When they deliver these Christmas baskets, they are often surprised by the apparent lack of gratitude on the part of the recipients. The young people are sometimes disillusioned by the fact that the people they are trying to help are indifferent, perhaps even hostile to them. These youth groups are given very little preparation for what they will encounter. They do not understand how humiliating it can be for the poor to be given food by a bunch of apparently spoiled rich kids who regard them as inferior.

Please do not think I am suggesting a curtailment of Christmas baskets to poor families. God knows that such gifts are needed and blessed. What I strongly suggest is that the deliveries be made in secret. It is a lot more *fun* to give in secret than to stroke your own ego by being obviously magnanimous. It *is* more blessed to give than to receive, but Jesus clearly teaches that when we give to the poor, it should be done with such secrecy that the recipients do not know from whence the gift comes. In Matthew 6:3–4, Jesus says "When thou doest alms, let not thy left hand know what thy right hand doeth: That thine alms may be in secret: and thy Father which seeth in secret himself shall reward thee openly."

An Even Better Thing to Do

Ron Sider, a colleague of mine at Eastern College, wrote a controversial book entitled *Rich Christians in an Age of Hunger*. This book makes what I believe to be an unshakable case for a simple lifestyle for Christians, clearly demonstrating from Scripture that God strongly identifies with the poor and the oppressed in their sufferings and that any who would be followers of Christ must share God's concern. Sider makes it obvious that the Kingdom of God is made up of people who do *not* view the accumulation of wealth as a desirable thing. He calls upon people to confront the radical teachings of Christ honestly and to be obedient in using their resources to meet the needs of the wretched of the earth.

Those who criticize Sider usually do so by claiming that he is technically naïve about economics. They think that he is calling for a simple redistribution of wealth in some kind of Christian communistic system. Such attacks reflect a misunderstanding of his position.

He agrees with his good friend John Perkins, author of *Let Justice Roll Down*, that if we redistributed the wealth, the rich would have it back very shortly. Sider realizes that the war on poverty cannot be carried out by a simple redistribution of wealth. All he is trying to communicate is that the relative indifference of rich Christians to the plight of the economically oppressed is unbiblical and sinful. In reality, his response to poverty has been much more pragmatic and realistic than his critics are ready to admit.

Recently, Sider joined with me and others at Eastern College to initiate a new master's degree program which is designed to train Christians to be what he calls "entrepreneurs for Biblical justice." The students in this program are trained to go in among the poor, both here in the urban ghettoes and in the slums of Third World countries, to help create cottage industries and small businesses. Sider believes that job creation is the best way of helping the poor. Those of us who are participants in this program believe that we can raise up a whole new generation of missionaries who will go in among the oppressed of the world and, with very limited resources, create jobs for them in the name of Christ. We use the following as our creed for economic development:

> Go to the people.
> Live among them.
> Learn from them.
> Plan with them.
> Build on what they have.
> Teach by showing.
> Learn by doing.
> Not a showcase, but a pattern.
> Not odds and ends, but a system.
> Not relief, but release.

Already our graduates are doing such things. One of them is in Kenya organizing a craft industry which will employ dozens of previously unemployed people. Another former student is bringing together welfare mothers in one of our large cities and is working with them to establish an array of small businesses that can make them economically independent. I could cite other examples, but I think I have made my point. We believe rich Christians must respond to the needs of the poor by financing economic development programs that enhance the dignity of those being helped and preserve their God-given humanity.

When we started this graduate program at Eastern,

there were many who said we would never get the young people of the '80s to enroll in a program that was not designed to make them rich. Happily, these skeptics have been proven wrong. New candidates are flocking to the program. The Christian community has many young people who would rather serve Christ among the poor than climb the corporate ladder. There are scores of young people who are not about to be seduced into a yuppie lifestyle, because they want to do something that will live on after they are dead. There are more and more young people who realize that serving Christ sacrificially is more *fun* than anything the world has to offer.

I met Mother Teresa once, and the thing that impressed me about her was not her piety, but her smile. The moment I saw her, I knew that she was enjoying life more than any yuppie ever could. Once, when a famous television commentator interviewed her in Calcutta, he said, "Mother Teresa, I wouldn't do what you're doing for all the money in the world." To which Mother Teresa answered, "Neither would I."

The concept is a paradox. Paul says in Philippians 3:8, ". . . I count all things but loss for the excellency of the knowledge of Christ Jesus, my Lord: for whom I have suffered the loss of all things, and do count them but dung, that I may win Christ."

Jesus calls us to service that offers us the kind of fulfillment that the world cannot understand. To everyone who has a thirst for the joyful suffering of Christ, He says—COME!

GETTING A KICK OUT OF WORK

The '60s were years in which everything in America changed. Our innocence was lost. The '60s took away "Leave It to Beaver" and gave us the Beatles. It was the decade that ended our political idealism and marked the emergence of a system of political expediency and manipulation. It left us wondering just how much of America is controlled by the CIA.

The youth of the tumultuous '60s felt increasingly powerless to change things on a global scale or, for that matter, on a national level. During that difficult decade, young people began to retreat into a subculture of their own making. More and more, they gave up on political action and sought refuge within the limited sphere of their own private lives. The cries for social reform faded and disillusioned hordes of youth began seeking individualized redemption in fads that ranged from sensitivity groups to est rather than hoping for the transformation of the politico-economic system.

As the years rolled on, young people determined that they would go to work, but only on their own terms. They decided that they would take positions within the business establishment, but they promised themselves that they would not sell their souls for bourgeois benefits. Their hope was to achieve some kind of personal Nirvana in which the inner longings of their hearts would be stilled because they had found some psychic peace.

Among the values of the counterculture that emerged from the ashes of Vietnam was the belief held by most young adults that one should not try to change the world until one's own head was together. It was important to the hippies and yippies of the late '60s and early '70s to gain one thing—a sense of personal satisfaction with life. Furthermore, they were convinced that one essential ingredient for the creation of a satisfying life was a job that offered a chance for self-expression. It seemed as if almost every student I talked to in those watershed years was looking for a job that would provide an emotional turn-on, "self-actualization," and "personal fulfillment." They believed that jobs that failed to deliver gratification should be rejected, regardless of what the pay might be. I can hear them now saying such things as, "Man, I have to be me on the job . . . *I mean*, if the job doesn't let me be me . . . I mean, if the job doesn't let me do my thing . . . I mean, if the job leaves me alienated without any psychic life. . . . I mean, who needs it? You know what I mean?"

So much of that counterculture lent itself to parody and ridicule, and yet, those young people had something to say that we should hear. Their message had value. In simple language, they asked if they could have jobs that they considered to be *fun*. Whereas previous generations joined labor unions to demand higher pay and job security, these long-haired, casually dressed moonbeam children told us that we should be looking for genuine fulfillment in our work.

The Joy of Creative Work

When my children were small, they enjoyed school mostly when they were given a chance to "make things." For them, the handcraft time at school was more treasured than recess. The times when they were given paper, crayons, and Elmer's Glue and told to make something special proved to be the highlights of their school experiences. It was always fun to welcome the kids home at the end of the day, have them hold up one of their precious creations, and hear them say proudly, "It's for you."

Their pictures were promptly displayed on the sides of the refrigerator. They were held there with little magnets, purchased especially for such purposes. Anything more bulky was neatly arranged on top of the refrigerator.

The fact that the work my children did in their craft time was such great fun for them inclines me to ask the question, "Shouldn't all work be fun? Shouldn't all work stimulate our creative juices and make our blood run hot with excitement? Is it asking too much of life to expect that our jobs be instruments for self-fulfillment and self-actualization?"

When I was a boy, my father worked at the RCA factory located in Camden, New Jersey. His wages were so low that it could be said that he was exploited. My father was a cabinet-maker back in the days when cabinets for radios were made by hand. While he worked for starvation wages, he did get something from his job that was more important than money. He got psychic gratification from his work. Making those cabinets was a real "turn-on" for him. He felt alive when he fashioned things of beauty out of wood. For him, what he produced was an extension of his ego. There was something mystical that he imparted to each cabinet he built. In a strange way, they were *his* cabinets. He would not get the profits from constructing them. He would not be given the recognition which he deserved for his craftsmanship. But he got something more—much more.

When we did our family visiting, which in the pre-TV era was a major form of entertainment, Dad would look for the radio in the house. If there was a console that was of his vintage, I would be given the responsibility of investigating. It was my assignment to get behind that big upright console and see if my father's initials were inscribed on it. My dad always initialed the back side of the cabinets he built. After all, they were *his* cabinets. *He* had made them. On two different occasions, I came across his initials, and when I did, he basked in self-satisfaction. And I had the feeling that I had the most creative, ingenious father in the world. My father had *fun* making radio cabinets. He had *fun* looking at the work of his hands.

In many ways, my father's job enabled him to imitate God. He, like Yahweh in Genesis 1:31, looked on all that he had created and saw that it was good. Shouldn't all human beings get something of the joy and satisfaction that God got out of His work? Even as God's creation allowed Him to express His personality, shouldn't our labors and vocational activities allow us to express our personalities? Shouldn't jobs that deny us the gratification of self-expression be rejected? Aren't these the questions that the young people who gave birth to the counterculture of the '60s ask of us?

The Importance of Job Satisfaction

Job satisfaction is crucial for the success of family life. A person who spends eight hours a day in a job that is emotionally draining and unfulfilling is a person who has a low libido level and is a lousy lover. If work dissipates the psychic energies of people, it renders them incapable of meaningful love relationships. If, at the end of a day, marital partners have a sick feeling that their lives are being wasted, it is difficult for them to come on to one another sexually. If work leaves people with a hollow feeling in the depths of their being then it is unlikely that they will have much enthusiasm about personal relationships. Countless divorces can be traced to vocational activities that left people dehumanized and emotionally dead.

Depression has become a malady that many people experience as a part of daily life. Any survey of workers in business and industry will reveal that a large number suffer regular bouts of depression. These workers, in interviews with researchers, make statements like the following: "I am really a nobody." "Nothing that I do really matters." "I get treated like dirt at work." "I have no fun at what I do all day." It is obvious that such negative feelings have a devastating influence on family life. Nobody enjoys being with depressed people. I am convinced that lack of fulfillment and the absence of fun on the job are responsible for more evil than can be measured.

G. K. Chesterton once wrote: "In the late afternoon, when the children tire of their games, it is then that they turn to torturing the cat."

It is easy to recognize the meaning of those lines. They make it very clear that when things become boring and are no longer fun for children, that will be just the time they will turn to mischievous and cruel behavior. The same is true for adults, but instead of torturing the cat, adults torture each other. Their attempts to allay the feelings of deadness that come from spending their days in unfulfilling work include adultery, wife-beating, brutalizing children, and other forms of evil. Sometimes they work little, yet come home exhausted. Their exhaustion comes not from physical exertion, but from a sense of meaninglessness and absence of the fulfillment of their creative powers.

The Protestant work ethic which dominated the American consciousness until the '60s put too much emphasis on working hard and accumulating wealth. Consequently, it was inevitable that sooner or later a reaction would occur. That reaction was part of what made the '60s such a strange decade of rebellion. There is some validity for the antithesis to the Protestant work ethic that was part of the counterculture of those years. The antiestablishment rebels of that period were simply repeating an ancient belief that "man doth not live by bread only."° They claimed that there must be more derived from a job than a salary. Their counterculture value system made them declare that work must be *fun*. It must be fun in the sense that it must leave them energized and capable of loving. It must be fun because life is too short to be spent doing the absurd and the meaningless. It must be fun because there is something very unchristian about despising one's employment. And I wholeheartedly concur.

Changing Attitudes instead of Changing Jobs

There are those who argue that a job change is not always possible or necessary in the quest for meaningful and fulfilling work. There are those who contend that sometimes it is best to bloom where you are planted. No doubt the poet John Milton was right when he said in *Paradise Lost*, "The mind is its own place."† Let me illustrate that point. A new worker at a factory asked his shop steward what it was like to work in this factory. The shop steward answered with a question of his own: "What was it like at your last job?" "Oh," said the new worker, "it was a miserable job. I didn't like the work and the bosses were unfair to me." "Unfortunately," responded the shop steward, "you'll find it much the same here."

° Deut. 8:3.
† Bk. 1, line 246.

Later, another new worker asked the same shop steward exactly the same question: "What is it like to work in this factory?" The shop steward once again answered with the counterquestion: "What was it like at your last job?" "Oh," said the new worker, "it was wonderful. The work was interesting, everybody was good to me. The working conditions were ideal." "Well," said the shop steward, "I'm happy to report that you will find this place just as wonderful as the last place where you worked."

The point of this little parable is obvious. People's dispositions often determine what they experience. There are some joyless people who would complain even if they were in heaven. There are those who, as Milton said, "can make a Hell of Heaven."*

The fact that what we *are* influences how we experience things provides another important reason for becoming a Christian. A conversion experience involves much more than simply accepting some doctrinaire truths about the work of Jesus. Being converted is undergoing what the sociologist Peter Berger calls an "alteration of personality." The converted individual views things in an entirely new way. The convert looks at the same events and realities, but everything means something different for the convert as a result of the transforming religious experience. According to Berger, the convert perceives things in an alternative fashion. In his second letter to the Christians at Corinth, the Apostle Paul put it this way: "Therefore, if any man be in Christ, he is a new creature: old things are passed away; behold all things are become new" (5:17).

* Bk. 1, line 255.

To be converted is to enter into a close personal relationship with the resurrected Jesus. The Christian experiences the world through the eyes of Christ and is in the process of being transformed into someone who thinks like Jesus.* This means that people you could not stand prior to conversion, you are capable of loving after conversion. It means that a job that might not have excited you because it did not pay well or seem prestigious becomes a channel through which you can serve others in the name of Christ. Becoming a Christian is establishing a relationship with a new friend and finding that the presence of this new friend inspires you to think and feel differently about everything.

One day when Christopher Wren, the English architect, was directing the construction of London's St. Paul's Cathedral, he stopped to talk to one of the laborers at the building site. "What do you do?" Wren inquired of the man. Not realizing that he was talking to the great architect, the man, who was a cement mixer, answered, "Sir, can't you see? I'm building a great cathedral." This humble worker had a perspective on his job that enabled him to view his work as having great significance. Some other cement mixer might have grudgingly responded, "Can't you see what I do? I mix this cement all day. It's not much of a job, but it's a living."

I know a woman who has a job as the Welcome Wagon lady of her community. She is hired to visit all new families that move into her township and give them packets of information explaining all the things the com-

---

* Phil. 2:5–7.

munity has to offer. She took the job because she was a single mother who needed work with flexible hours that would allow her to be available when her two daughters needed her. However, the job often left her depressed. She had been deserted by her husband, and her job involved visiting intact families that reminded her of what she had lost.

One day while making a visit to a new family, she encountered a Christian couple who shared their knowledge of Christ with her. She accepted the invitation to become a Christian, and her conversion changed her whole attitude toward her job. Instead of viewing it only as a necessary means of making her house payments and feeding her family, she began to see that her job offered all kinds of possibilities for Christian service. She often had the chance to counsel people about their problems, and on many occasions she was able to share her new-found faith through personal testimony. Her job became an excellent opportunity to direct people into the ministries of the various churches in the community. And after awhile, others began to notice. In fact, her contributions attracted so much attention that the ministers' council of the township gave her a special award recognizing her outstanding Christian service to the community. This woman did not change jobs; she changed attitudes.

Unfortunately, conversion does not always make us happy in our work. Each of us is different. God has given to each person unique gifts which, in turn, create unique interests. A particular job may offer great possibilities for Christian service and creative labor, but the person in that job may not be made for that sort of work. It is easy to be misplaced. It is easy to end up in a job that is not for you. The counterculture types of the '60s understood this and told the rest of us we should make a change if some other job had greater possibilities for personal fulfillment.

The value system of the counterculture of the '60s in regard to work can be summarized as follows:

1. Make sure your job turns you on. If it does not, quit and try to find some other job that does. If your job does not provide fulfillment, you will be a tense and emotionally dead person who will make life miserable for everybody around you.

2. Know what your "thing" is. You have to know what gifts and interests you have in order to find a job that is fun for you. Make sure your job gives you a chance to express yourself.

3. Make sure what is going on in your own head is okay. If your personal relationships are messed up or you, yourself, are messed up psychologically, *no* job will be fun for you.

These are not bad guidelines, but I am convinced that there is more to finding fulfilling work than these ideas suggest.

Going by the Bible

The Bible also promises personal fulfillment. The message of Christ has all kinds of references to how to be happy and full of fun. However, the Biblically prescribed means to achieving fulfillment is diametrically opposed to most of what emerges from the work philosophies of both the culture and counterculture. The Bibli-

cal way to personal joy and to a fun-loving approach to
life stands in marked contrast to what the world in general prescribes. Whereas the yuppies of the '80s say that
we will be satisfied with life if we work hard, make a lot
of money, and become financially secure, Jesus showed
us another perspective. In His "Parable of the Rich
Fool," He tells us of a man who did just that—planning
bigger barns and better leisure time. And then, of course,
he died and all that he planned was for nothing. And God
said to the rich man:

> "Thou fool, this night thy soul shall be required of thee:
> then whose shall those things be, which thou hast pro-
> vided?" So is he that layeth up treasure for himself, and is
> not rich toward God.[*]

Whereas the counterculture of the '60s argues that the
thirst for happiness should drive us to find ourselves and
to live for our own self-actualization, the Bible in Matthew 16:25 teaches us that people who try to find themselves will lose themselves. "For whosoever will save his
life shall lose it: and whosoever will lose his life for my
sake shall find it."

The Bible teaches that living for Christ, which is actually living sacrificially for others, promises joyful personal fulfillment. The way to satisfaction in life as taught
in the Scriptures is through self-giving and service.
Happy living, according to the Christian message, comes
through loving God and committing ourselves to doing
His work in the world.

[*] Luke 12:20–21.

We Are Made in the Likeness of One Who Likes His Work

The Creator of the universe enjoys His work. At the end of each day of Creation, He sat back and looked at what He produced and, with genuine satisfaction, told Himself repeatedly how good His creations were.* God created what He did because it brought Him joy. He expressed Himself in His creation, and all that He created glorified Him.

Lord Chesterton suggested that God got a childlike excitement out of His work. As a matter of fact, he contended that God may be the only one left in the universe who has childlike emotions about work, while all the rest of us have grown old and cynical because of sin. God never tires of what He does. He enjoys it all.

If you take a five-year-old child, throw her into the air, catch her, bounce her off your knee, and then set her down on the floor, you can expect her to exclaim, "Do it again!" Every time you do it, she will shout with even more enthusiasm, "Do it again!" If you repeat the process a dozen times, the child will not tire of these antics.

Lord Chesterton believed that God may be that way about creating daisies. He asks us to imagine God creating the first daisy and enjoying it so much that something down inside Him exclaims, "Do it again!" And when He makes the second daisy, He is even more excited and shouts to Himself, "Do it again!" Imagine God

---

* Gen. 1:4, 10, 12, 18, 21, 25.

continuing to create daisy after daisy, and after making the hundred-billionth daisy being even more filled with excitement than when He began. Obviously, this is an exaggeration but it makes no difference. The principle is what is valid—God is a God who delights in what He does.

If we are created in the image of a God who enjoys His work, then failing to delight in our work is a denial of part of what we are supposed to be. It is the responsibility of each of us to become more and more like God. "Be ye therefore perfect, even as your Father which is in heaven is perfect" (Matt. 5:48). Being like God implies deriving joy from our work.

A good job is one that allows the worker the privilege of self-giving. God is a self-giver. In John 3:16, we learn the extent of His giving work on our behalf: "For God so loved the world that he gave his only begotten Son, that whosoever believeth in him should not perish, but have everlasting life." Consequently, those people who give of themselves for others in the work that they do are in the process of becoming what God expects them to be.

I know an insurance salesman who, for years, viewed his clients only as a means to make money. However, one day this salesman came into a personal, saving relationship with Christ. His attitude changed, and he began to view his work as an opportunity to serve others in the name of Jesus. After his conversion, when he talked to people about purchasing insurance policies, he approached them on the basis of meeting a need in their lives. After selling a policy, he continued to express loving concern toward his clients. When death struck, he not only delivered the pay-off check, but he also visited the bereaved family and tried to offer consolation. As his work became far more to him than a means of making money, he found more and more fulfillment in what he was doing. As he turned his job into a mission of self-giving in the name of Christ, he came to know job satisfaction as never before.

M. Scott Peck, the famous Christian psychotherapist, tells an interesting story that demonstrates that people often refuse to have joy in life and fun at their jobs because serving other people appears to be a big bother. He tells of a young woman who became one of his patients. This particular woman was suffering from acute depression and was failing to respond to any form of therapy or other treatment. Dr. Peck was just about to give up on this case when the young woman surprised him one day bouncing into his office, her face aglow with excitement. When he asked her why she was feeling so good, the young woman explained that on the way to her appointment she had enjoyed a very happy experience. She explained that her car had broken down so she had called her pastor and asked if he could help her get to her therapy appointment. Her pastor told her that he would be glad to drive her to her appointment if she did not mind his making a few hospital calls on the way. When the pastor got to the hospital, he invited her to go in with him and then suggested that she spend her waiting time visiting and praying with some of the patients. She told how she visited several patients and tried to speak words of encouragement to them. She prayed with several of the patients, and they, in turn, showed great appreciation for her concern. It was this self-giving service that had given her such an emotional lift.

Dr. Peck then pointed out the good news. They now knew what she could do to keep from being depressed. Surprisingly, the young woman responded, "You don't expect me to do that every day, do you?!" She knew what to do to get rid of her depression and to make her life fun, and yet she refused to do it. But before we become too surprised at her foolishness, should we not ask whether many of us have made similar decisions? Is it not true that many of us are too lazy to do those self-giving deeds that would make our lives fun?

I know an accountant who hated his job. His wife has often spoken to me about how depressed he is because of what his job is doing to him. In an attempt to get him to experience a change of scene for a few weeks, I suggested that he accompany me on a trip I had to make to the mission field. I pointed out that the mission post I was visiting had all kinds of accounting problems and that he probably could render some valuable help.

Things turned out better than I had expected. The missionaries welcomed his services with open arms. Day after day, he straightened out messes and set things in proper order. His face literally glowed with excitement and joy. When it was time for him to leave, he hated to go home. Furthermore, the missionaries pleaded with him to join them on an ongoing basis. They pointed out that there were other missionary organizations like theirs that needed his help and that his contribution for some of these organizations might be crucial for their survival.

But when all was said and done, it was mostly said. While he was intrigued with the offer, he turned it down. His wife would have been thrilled to go to the mission field with him. He could have had a job which would have been fun for him. But in the end, he turned down what would have made him a happy person and returned to a job that he despised. He thought he had done the reasonable thing, but there is nothing more unreasonable than rejecting what could have been an enjoyable, fun job to settle for a yuppie job that was spiritually and psychologically draining.

Meeting God in Other People

Serving others is the ultimate way to achieve joy and fulfillment for Christians. Those who serve will learn that they can encounter God through those whom they serve. I can attest to the fact that on more than one occasion I gained a sense of mystical transcendence when loving and serving a person in the name of Christ. On such occasions it is as though Christ Himself is reaching out to me through the needy person to whom I am reaching out in love. Service to others is a blessing to me because every person who is served is transfigured in my mind into the Jesus who gave Himself for me. I believe that Jesus uses needy people in a sacramental way and allows me to touch Him when I touch them. The person who confronts me is not Jesus, and yet I meet Jesus through participating in the life of that person.

There is a true story of a boy who suffered under the Nazis during World War II that clearly communicates what I am trying to put into words. This Jewish boy was living in a small Polish village when he and all the other Jews of the vicinity were rounded up by Nazi SS Troops and sentenced to death. This boy joined his neighbors in digging a shallow ditch for their graves. Then they were lined up against a wall and machine-gunned. Their corpses fell into the shallow grave and then the Nazis covered their crumpled bodies with dirt. But none of the bullets hit this little boy. His naked body was splattered with the blood of his parents and when they fell into the ditch, he pretended to be dead and fell on top of them. The grave was so shallow that the thin covering of dirt did not prevent air from getting through to him so that he could breathe.

Several hours later, when darkness fell, this ten-year-old boy clawed his way out of the grave. With blood and dirt caked to his little body, he made his way to the nearest house and begged for help. Recognizing him as one of the Jewish boys marked for death by the SS, the woman who answered screamed at him to go away and slammed the door. He was turned away at the next house as well as at the one after that. In each case, the unwillingness to risk getting into trouble with the SS Troops overpowered any feeling of compassion that these people might have had. Dirty, bloodied, and shivering, the little boy limped from one house to the next begging for somebody to help him. Then something inside seemed to guide him to say something that was very strange for a Jewish boy to say. When the next family responded to his timid knocking in the still of the night, they heard him cry, "Don't you recognize me? I am the Jesus you say you love." After a poignant pause that must have seemed like an eternity to the little boy, the woman who stood in the doorway swept him into her arms and kissed him. From that day on, the members of that family cared for that boy as though he was one of their own.

This story was told by the woman who took him in on

that horrible night. She told the story not to elicit praise for herself, but to tell others of the joy and happiness he had brought to her over the years. She had discovered that when one labors to help hurting people, one labors to serve Jesus Himself. What could be more fulfilling work than that?

One day during the week before Christmas, I was heading into John Wanamaker's, a fine department store in Philadelphia. I was planning to buy some presents for my family. Sitting on a wooden box, just to the side of the store's entrance, was a woman who appeared to be mentally retarded. There was a dullness in her face, and her general demeanor suggested that she just did not have it all together. Two policemen standing on either side of her were comforting her because she was desperately crying. She was repeating in singsong fashion, "Dem boys, dem boys, dem bad, bad boys. Dey took my money. Dey took my money and now Agnes got no money for Christmas." She moaned her story to everyone who passed by. The two policemen did their best to calm her, but there was nothing they could do that could allay her pain. She had been robbed of her money, and so her dreams for Christmas were shattered.

I had forty dollars in my pocket, and I suddenly had the urge to take that money and squeeze it into her hands. But I didn't. I went into the store to buy my presents and left her sitting on that wooden box in the hands of the two sweet and concerned policemen.

By the time I got to the center of the store, I realized what I had failed to do. I turned and ran back to where that strange woman had been sitting so that I could give her the money—but she was gone. I hurried up and down the streets around the store, but I could not find her.

That evening, I called the police station to see if they had any record of the woman, but they had no record of her at all. It was as though she had vanished without a trace. Then I remembered the admonition in Hebrews 13:1–3:

> Let brotherly love continue. Be not forgetful to entertain strangers: for thereby some have entertained angels unawares. Remember them that are in bonds, as bound with them; and them which suffer adversity, as being yourselves also in the body.

I realized that I had missed a chance to serve angels or, even worse, I had missed a chance to serve my Lord. Oh, what joy we often forfeit!

The Best Reason to Work

The Protestant work ethic puts a great emphasis on working hard and accumulating a lot of money. This value system makes us into hard-working people, and that is good. However, the accumulation of wealth does not deliver the emotional gratification that many of us think it will. I guess I agree with John Wesley when he said, "Christians should work as hard as they can in order to make as much money as they can in order to give away all they can." I guess it's okay to make the accumulation of wealth your life's goal, particularly if you plan to give a good bit of it away in the name of Christ. But I believe it is even better when the work itself is a service to God. I think that when you can view your work as a means of helping others in the name of Christ, you will have more fun at what you do. Why not take stock of your life and ask yourself if you are doing what you ought to be doing? Why not ask yourself if the time has come for you to give more than your money to God? Why not ask if your work, not just your salary, can be offered up to God as service for His Kingdom?

Second, working for personal satisfaction certainly seems like a reasonable thing to do. But I think that in most cases, those who seek personal gratification never really find it. I think that personal gratification is much like a dog's tail. If the dog chases it, the dog goes around in circles, but if the dog goes purposefully about its business, the tail just follows along behind. I believe that people who make personal happiness a goal seldom reach that goal. Strange as it may seem, people have fun in what they do if they forget the money they will be paid and forget their longings for personal gratification, and instead, singlemindedly seek to make their lives a sacrificial offering for others. I believe that to live for Christ is to gain the joyful aliveness and fulfillment that the world so desperately seeks but never finds. If you believe that your job is the best way available to you for maximizing your service to others in the name of Christ, you will be satisfied with life. There may be a lot of pain and sacrifice in serving Christ, but there's a lot of fun in it, too.

Part Three
_____

IN FAMILY LIFE

HOLDING TOGETHER IN A WORLD THAT'S FALLING APART

Building successful families is an increasingly difficult job. There is no need to rehearse the statistics that prove that divorce is a widespread epidemic and that parents are unable to control the behavior of their children. We no longer hear the suggestions of the avant-garde intelligentsia that oppressive sexual standards and archaic family structures are being abandoned in favor of freer and more humanizing practices. Everyone now is aware of the fact that what Americans are experiencing is not a transition into some kind of a brave new world, but a total collapse of society's most basic institution. The once common claims that children of divorced parents are just as likely to make healthy psychological adjustments to life as are children from intact families have been proven false. We now know that the more than 50 percent of America's children who have had to endure the breakup of their parents' marriages carry with them deep emotional scars. We all know that these fractured families are creating unparalleled agony for millions of children.

The mere declaration that family solidarity is a good thing and that old-fashioned sexual standards are best will not solve our problems. We must go beyond the rhetoric that calls for a return to traditional family values. We must do more than talk about what ought to be. We must *do* something now to reestablish the kind of healthy families in which people can have fun. We must figure out what we can *do* to make marriages work. We must realize that, like Humpty Dumpty, the institution of the family in America has had a great fall, and the time has come to do those things which will put it back together again.

Ritual and Group Solidarity

Emile Durkheim, the famous French sociologist, taught that ritual is essential for the health and maintenance of any social institution. We now know that what he had to say about ritual is particularly relevant to the family. We know that people optimize happiness in the context of families that have healthy solidarity, and Durkheim teaches that ritual is a powerful means for generating that solidarity. Durkheim's theories suggest that families with high levels of ritual will have more stable marriages and healthy children than those with low levels of ritual. In the absence of consistent ritual, families tend to fall apart morally and psychologically.

Actually, Durkheim argues that there are four ways that rituals contribute to the life of a group. His claims about ritual are as follows:

1. It enhances the solidarity of the group.
2. It builds loyalty to the values of the group.
3. It communicates the values of the group to new members.
4. It creates a euphoric sense of well-being for the members of the group.

Ritual and Religion

When the word *ritual* is mentioned, people tend to think of religion. It is in religious worship that ritual is most evident. Churches that have a great deal of ritual, as is the case with those in the Roman Catholic, Episcopal, and Lutheran traditions, tend to have more loyal members and more stability than those that are less ritualistic, like the Baptist and the Assemblies of God.

Nonliturgical churches which embrace a free-wheeling evangelistic style of worship may grow rapidly, but that growth is often unstable. I have watched such churches thrive under the leadership of dynamic preachers, and then collapse quickly when those preachers leave. Such successes are almost completely determined by the charisma of those who occupy their pulpits.

An Assembly of God church in our neighborhood grew from a cottage prayer meeting to a congregation of thousands in the course of just a few years. Then, when the pastor moved to another charge, a less dynamic preacher was called. The church rapidly declined in size, experienced two schisms, and eventually became so small that it had to disband and sell its buildings.

Liturgical churches normally show more stability than that. Roman Catholic churches, for instance, tend to be more solid and to have members who are more dependable. It is all well and good if the priest in a given parish gives brilliant homilies, but even if he should be replaced by some prosaic plodder, the people of that congregation will continue to attend mass and to support their church. The liturgy has a psychological hold on them, and they demonstrate the Durkheimian principle that ritual encourages loyalty and builds solidarity.

As a matter of fact, the Roman Catholic community in our day is facing one of its most serious challenges because of the recent decline of ritual in the mass. Since Vatican II, more experimentation and innovation have been permitted in the mass. In some instances, individual congregations have developed worship services which almost seem to resemble Protestant services. There are hymn singing, gospel preaching, and masses in English rather than in Latin. Just a few decades ago, Catholics could attend church almost anywhere in the world on a given Sunday and the liturgy would be like that of every church everywhere. But this uniformity seems to have disappeared. With the demise of a unifying, prescribed ritual, there has come a breakdown of the monolithic quality of Roman Catholicism. Nowadays, Catholicism seems to come in all shapes and forms. When Catholics move from church to church, they never can be sure of what to expect. There are all kinds of Catholic churches ranging from those led by Pentecostal priests to those led by priests who are into liberation theology.

The variations in the liturgy and the decline of ritual has had its effect upon the attendance at Catholic churches, too. Catholics—particularly elderly Catholics—have demonstrated less and less enthusiasm for attending mass. One of my Italian relatives, once a very regular worshiper at mass, often stays away from church these days. When I asked him why he was absent from church so often, he responded in his heavy Italian accent, "Hey, it's not the same. Last time I went to that church, there was some hippie priest up front with a guitar. He was singing some crazy jazzy song. I don't know what's goin' on at that place anymore. At the end of the mass, the priest said, 'Turn and greet your neighbor with a holy kiss.' When the guy next to me looked at me, I said, 'You stay away or I'm gonna punch in your face.'"

While mass in the vernacular fosters a clearer presentation of the gospel, it must be noted that, with the end of the traditional ritual, something precious was lost. As a consequence, some Catholics are less loyal and others no longer *feel* the same about mass.

Jews are even more ritualistic than Catholics. With Orthodox Jews, ritual is not only evident in worship, but it is evident throughout every aspect of their daily lives. In the musical *Fiddler on the Roof*, the main character, Tevye, opens the show by explaining to the audience what makes Jews Jewish. He claims that it is tradition. His hit song "Tradition" explains that for true Jews, there are traditional rituals for every human activity.

There are rituals for eating, dressing, and for doing business. There are traditions for matchmaking and for marriage. There are established ways of doing almost anything which is a part of Jewish life. Tevye explains to the audience that the traditions which are expressed in these multiple rituals give stability to Jewish existence. Without their rituals and traditions, he shouts, their lives would be as shaky as "a fiddler on a roof."

Anyone who has studied the Jewish culture knows how important the rituals are. It is their rituals which have generated such a unified consciousness among Jews. If war breaks out in the Middle East, Jews everywhere feel involved and rally to the support of the state of Israel. In spite of being scattered all over the world since Biblical days, they have never really lost their identity. Jews have never forgotten who they are and to whom they belong. Their ritual helps them to retain their identity.

Family life among Jews is stronger than it is among some other ethnic groups because their families are so steeped in traditional rituals. The major holy days of Judaism are not celebrated in the synagogue as much as they are in the family. For instance, the Seder feast is celebrated in the home with the expressed purpose of teaching the children about the travail of the Jews in Egypt and their deliverance through the Exodus. Each of the foods eaten in the feast symbolizes some part of this agonizing and glorious chapter of Jewish history. Through the ritual, all Jewish children grow up knowing about their roots and learning to be loyal to their ethnic brothers and sisters.

When I taught at the University of Pennsylvania, a

great number of my students were Jewish. When the time of the Seder approached, many of them would come to me and explain that they were going to be absent from class because of the Jewish holy days. On one occasion, some students asked to be excused whom I knew to be avowed atheists. When I suggested that I did not see the point of excusing atheists to celebrate a religious holiday, one of them responded with a hint of anger, "We may be atheists, but we are still Jewish."

It is interesting to note that the Seder is so overtly designed to enhance family solidarity and to communicate Jewish values to children that the feast cannot be properly celebrated without their presence. Consequently, my Jewish students would sometimes ask if they could borrow my children in order to properly celebrate the occasion. And I readily agreed.

An encounter with Muslims will still any doubt about the ability of ritual to bind people together and endow them with group values. Recently I visited Senegal, a Muslim nation in West Africa and saw firsthand why missionaries have such a difficult time trying to convert Islamic people to Christianity.

Five times each day all Muslim believers are called to prayer. Wherever they are, the faithful get down on their knees, bow towards Mecca, and praise the name of Allah. Five times a day they ritualistically reaffirm their commitment to their faith and to their Muslim values. Each time they are psychologically recommitted to their Muslim brothers and sisters around the world. It is easy to see why it is so difficult to convert a Muslim or even to shake his loyalty to Islam.

Jesus and Ritual

Jesus understood the importance of ritual, and He used it well to maintain the values and truths essential for the survival of His Church. Central to His mission in the world was His death and resurrection. Crucial to His Church is the remembrance of His saving acts of grace. Because of the importance of these things, Jesus did more than tell His followers to remember His death until He returned in glory. Instead, He wrapped up the memory of the cross in the ritual of Holy Communion. Whenever the Lord's Supper is celebrated by Christians, His followers are reminded that His body was broken for them and that His blood was shed for the remission of their sins.

Jesus was asking for literal obedience when He said, "This do . . . in remembrance of me. For as often as ye eat this bread, and drink this cup, ye do shew the Lord's death till he come."* He knew that if His followers did not ritualistically celebrate the Lord's Supper, they would be likely to forget what His death was all about, and that the frequent repetition of the ritual would keep the cross central in their theology.

Ritual in Family Life

Some families are much concerned with ritual. They have set, elaborate prescriptions for how holidays and birthdays should be celebrated. They have rules and expectations about behavior and conversation at meals.

* 1 Cor. 11:25–26.

134

Sometimes they even establish a pattern of vacationing in the same places or doing the same things each year.

Those families that have a great deal of ritual are usually the ones that are the most solid and secure. They seem better able to impart to their children the values and truths which they believe to be of ultimate significance. Ritualistic families have proportionately fewer juvenile delinquents, and their children are psychologically more healthy. Rituals are good for families, and instituting rituals makes family life more fun for everyone.

In our family, birthdays are very special. It is a major sin among us for anyone to fail to send a card to the birthday person. There are presents given at breakfast and a birthday cake at the evening meal. The birthday person can choose what food the family will eat for dinner, and there is always the singing of the "Happy Birthday" song. Our children grew up believing that everybody celebrated birthdays this way. It came as something of a surprise to them to learn that for some children a birthday is just another day and passes with little recognition. They could not believe that for many of their friends birthdays were not a big deal.

Christmas Rituals

Christmas always has been a ritual-filled day in the Campolo family. Our children always woke up earlier on Christmas morning, and once awake, they could not wait to get on with the opening of presents. However, there was a prescribed ritual for the opening of gifts. The children were not allowed to leave their rooms until my wife and I got up, and on Christmas morning, that was never until eight o'clock. Until eight o'clock, they could play with the little things we had stuffed in stockings that were hung by their beds. But they could never get to the "good stuff" under the Christmas tree until my wife and I had called them out of their rooms. Then they knew that before we could open presents, we would have to march right through the living room, into the kitchen, and have breakfast. If you wonder how it was possible to get excited children to have breakfast before opening presents on Christmas morning, I can only say, "We *always* did it that way." It was a ritual.

After breakfast, we would take our places in the living room, and Bart, our youngest, would go to the pile of presents under the tree, pick one and then give it to my wife, who would read the tag aloud. Then Bart would give it to the person whose name was on the tag. The recipient would slowly open the gift while the rest of us looked on, cheered, and made guesses as to what the gift might be. Then we would go through the same ritual with the second present and so on.

Our gift-opening sometimes took hours. I think it is really sad that children are allowed to dive unceremoniously into their presents, tear away the wrappings, and end the surprises of Christmas in just a couple of minutes. When that happens, they miss the drama that ritual can create. They miss the exciting anticipation as everyone wonders who will be getting the gift that is in the big box at the bottom of the pile.

In the afternoons, we always visited my mother and then my in-laws. Visiting our children's grandparents was deliberately made into a ritual because I know that someday I will be a grandparent and I will eagerly await visits from my children's families. I feel sure that they will come to visit me because visiting parents on Christmas day has become part of our family ritual.

Thanksgiving Day Rituals

The most ritualistic day in American life is Thanksgiving Day. More people return home to be with their families for this day than for any other holiday of the year. Those who travel as much as I do know that plane reservations must be secured well in advance for Thanksgiving time. Planes are jammed with people longing to get home to their families in order to ritualistically reaffirm their commitments and once again to revitalize a sense of belonging.

On Thanksgiving Day, a typical American family plans to eat the big dinner at approximately the same time each year. The menu is always the same, with turkey, dressing, and cranberry sauce heading the list. Each year, people seem to make the same comments about the food, the table, the children. It all may seem a bit corny and perhaps even unnecessary until one day the ritual comes to an end.

One day your son calls from college and you call your wife to the extension phone. After the usual pleasantries and the customary bit of joking you say, "Well, kid, three more weeks and you'll be home for Thanksgiving."

There's a poignant pause and then he says, "That's one of the reasons I'm calling, Dad. It's been a tough semester, a lot of tension. I've really been hitting the books real hard. So some of the guys and I thought we'd take off for Fort Lauderdale for the Thanksgiving break. That way, we can relax, have some fun, and take in some rays."

The news is greeted with stillness. And then your wife says, with hurt in her voice, "But . . . but . . . we *always* have Thanksgiving together."

"Look," he says, "it's not the end of the world. I'll be home for the long Christmas break in just a few weeks."

But it is the end of the world. It is the end of that precious world called the immediate family which you and your wife neatly and carefully constructed over the years. Neither you nor your wife may have read Emile Durkheim's books about the role of ritual in the maintenance of group solidarity, but you both know that something of great significance is about to be changed; something precious is about to end.

That Thanksgiving, the whole family, save one, will come together. You will all sit down at the same table to eat the same food, prepared in exactly the same way. And yet, deep down inside you will know that nothing ever will be the same again. You will eat the meal while pretending that nothing has changed. You will try to keep the talk light and happy, but it just won't work. Halfway through the meal, a pall of silence will fall over you all, and someone will say, "You know, it's just not the same." Nothing could be closer to the truth, and you will know it. You will have a painful awareness that nothing will ever be the same again.

The ritual has been broken, and the end of the ritual signals the end of an era. It is time for new families to begin with their own rituals. It is time for parents to recognize that they are approaching that stage of life when they have only each other to depend upon. The breaking of the ritual is a painful rite of passage that produces inner pain.

Ritual Revitalizes the Past

Ritual makes what happened a long time ago contemporaneous in our consciousness. It helps us to recall feelings that otherwise would get lost in the past. Nowhere is the revitalizing of the past through ritual more evident to me than in weddings.

At Eastern College, the Christian liberal arts school where I teach, I am often asked by students if I would perform their wedding ceremony. When my schedule permits me to do so, I take great pleasure in participating in these important occasions. However, I get a bit testy if my students tell me that they have abandoned the traditional wedding rituals and have invented rituals of their own. When I marry people, I try to persuade them to use the old forms and ceremonies that are set forth in the Book of Common Prayer.

There are those who say, "They are the ones getting married. They should have the kind of ceremony that is meaningful to them." To such remarks I can only respond by saying that such a perspective shows far too limited an understanding of what weddings are all about. While it is true that the couple in the front of the church is being married, it should be understood that, if the ceremony is properly constructed, those in the pews may go through a symbolic process of being remarried at the same time. When we attend weddings in which we hear the same words repeated that we ourselves uttered when we were married, we experience a sense of marital renewal.

When I hear a young man saying the same words that I said myself more than a quarter of a century ago, I seem to go through that same ceremony of commitment once again. When he says, "I, John, take thee, Mary, to be my wife; And I do promise and covenant; Before God and these witnesses; To be thy loving and faithful husband . . . ," I can hear myself saying, "I, Tony, take thee, Peggy, to be my wife; And I do promise and covenant. . . ." It all comes back to me in the ritual. The past is renewed. I feel the feelings of my wedding day. I sense the commitment I made on that day, and my marriage is renewed.

As a boy growing up in a very ethnically conscious Italian family, I was required to attend countless weddings and funerals. Both were great fun—yes, even the funerals. Looking back on my upbringing, I wonder just how much I was affected by my constant participation in those ceremonies. I wonder how much those rituals helped establish my identity as an Italian and how much they endowed me with a value system of love and respect. I now believe the influence of those rituals to have been very great indeed in forming who I am.

Ritual and Christian Nurture

When I was part of the sociology faculty of the University of Pennsylvania, I had an atheistic colleague who once said to me sarcastically, "The family that prays together stays together, even if there is no God." In spite of his antireligious world-view, my colleague recognized that rituals such as regular family devotions enhance the solidarity of a family. While he did not believe that there is a God who hears prayers, he was convinced that a family who has a set time for prayers and maintains a set pattern for Bible readings is engaging in ritualistic patterns that build family loyalty. Furthermore, he believed that such rituals as family devotions provide one of the most effective means for encouraging children to make a commitment to the basic values of the Christian faith.

It is important for Christians to take note of the unbiased observations of my atheistic friend. Children seldom learn from such direct approaches as lecturing or admonishing. Parents who have ever tried to tell their children what is right and what is wrong can attest to this.

I can remember telling my son, in no uncertain terms, why his failure to straighten up his room each day would lead to his downfall in life. He sat with his head bowed and his eyes fixed on the cat during my tirade. After I told him fervently of the importance of being a responsible person and not having to be reminded constantly to do what he should do, he asked meekly, "Can I leave now?" And I realized that nothing I said had sunk in.

Family rituals, on the other hand, have a latent effect on children which ultimately commits them to family values and makes them want subconsciously to do the things that good family members do. Children from highly ritualistic families have an intense longing to identify with

their families, and this longing leads them to find pleasure in doing those things that their families deem right.
From a sociological point of view, parents who do not
plan to have regular family devotions fail to take advantage of a practice that could mean the difference between having children who *want* to be loyal to the values
and beliefs of their parents and children who readily
abandon such values and beliefs.

Sometimes parents try to justify not having regular
family devotions. They claim that their children do not
enjoy family devotions and that they always give them a
hard time when asked to participate in Bible study and
prayer. I respond to such arguments by pointing out that
the participants do not have to like a given ritual for that
ritual to have a positive psychological effect upon them.
Rituals can build loyalty and commitment to family values regardless of the attitude of those who are involved
in performing them.

Rituals and Psychological Well-Being

I do not want to convey the impression that disliking
ritual is a normal reaction among children, for the opposite is true. Actually, family rituals, particularly
those which are religious in nature, are enjoyed by
most children. In most instances, family rituals create a
sense of well-being among children, and help them to
feel secure.

When my children were small, there were special rituals accompanying their bedtime. My children loved these
rituals and would have been very upset if they had not
been observed. Every night, after tucking them in, we

listened to their prayers. Then, as my wife and I would begin to leave their room, they would yell, "Drinks!"

I have found that there is no way to prevent children from crying for drinks when they have been put to bed. You may pour a gallon of water into them prior to tucking them in, but they will still beg for drinks. It is a ritual, and rituals are based on psychological hunger rather than on physical need.

When my wife had gotten a glass of water for each of them, she would ask, "How much?"

The children would then shout, "Two gulps and a swallow!" You could count on their saying just those words because they were part of the nightly ritual.

After each of them had taken "two gulps and a swallow," my wife and I would once again head for the door, and once again they would yell, but this time they would want me to sing "Wiggle Down." "Wiggle Down" is a little song I made up to the tune of a university fight song. It goes like this:

> Wiggle down, Bart and Lisa, wiggle down.
> You can sleep, Bart and Lisa,
> if you'll only wiggle down.
> You can sleep, Bart and Lisa,
> You can sleep, Bart and Lisa,
> You can sleep, Bart and Lisa,
> If you'll only wiggle down.

When I finished the song, the children would always cheer, and my wife and I would leave their room for the night. They then went off to sleep, convinced that God was in His heaven and all was right with the world. The rituals had generated a level of psychic well-being that diminished the possibility of nightmares and gave them a sense that their world was still ordered as it should be, that nothing essential had changed.

A child may have had a shattering day. He or she may have been scolded by a teacher, suffered unbearable humiliation at the hands of some bully, or been rejected by a friend. Who can tell what really goes on at school? Asking any child what happened at school on a given day will usually elicit the answer, "Nothing!" And yet that child may have been wounded emotionally, but just not be willing to talk about it.

The good thing about ritual is that it can put a child's shattered world back together again. A ritual before the lights are turned out, such as the one just described, can convince a child that the world is still in order and that everything is okay.

There are so few things that can be controlled in a child's life these days that parents who neglect the use of ritual have neglected one of the few available instruments for building emotional security and loyalty to family values. When parents ask me how they can help their children to overcome insecurities, I answer, "Ritual!" When they ask me how they can get their children to embrace the right kind of behavior patterns, I say, "Ritual!" When parents ask how they can give their children good feelings about themselves, I say, "Ritual!"

Tevye was right. Without ritual, children forget what they should remember and lose sight of what they should believe. Without traditions, children fail to learn how to behave. Without ritual, they become as shaky "as . . . as . . . as . . . a fiddler on a roof."

I am an evangelical Baptist. As such, I have been inclined in the past to underestimate the value of ritual. That may have been one of my most serious errors in judgment. Those of us in nonliturgical traditions would do well to discover the importance of ritual, not only in religion, but in all of life. What we do not understand may lead to our downfall.

WHAT THE WORLD NEEDS NOW IS LOVE, SWEET LOVE

Rituals build solidarity. Rituals generate loyalty. Rituals create a sense of well-being. Rituals remind us of things we must not forget. But rituals are no substitute for love. The Bible not only calls us to respect ritual, but it also calls us to discover the ways and power of love. Without love, life is not much fun. Without love, certainly marriage is no fun.

Love, according to the Bible, is something that we *do*. While there is no denial that there is a feeling that should accompany love, the Bible commands us to view love as *a commitment to do for others those things that will help them to become what God wants them to be.* Matthew 5:44 calls upon us to love our enemies, Luke

12:31 to love our neighbors, and John 15:2 to love one another. And then in Ephesians 5:25 husbands are commanded to love their wives. In each instance the Biblical writers make it clear that love is a commitment to action.

The idea that love is something we do is somewhat foreign to the modern Western mind. We are the people who grew up thinking that love is a feeling that overtakes a person when that person meets "the right one." If any of you should ask your mother, "How will I know if I have met the right one?," your mother will probably answer, "When you meet the right one—*you'll know!*"

In our romantically oriented culture, we are socialized to believe that love is an irrational emotion over which we have no control. Love, we are told, is something into which we "fall." And everyone is led to believe that when a person "falls in love," he or she can expect to live happily ever after.

It is no wonder that so many marriages fail. People don't understand that it entails hard work to maintain love, and that love is not a natural happening. They do not take hold of the fact that love is something we are called to do, and that love requires commitment, concern, and concentration.

Being Misled by the Greeks

We who live in the Western world have been led to these false conceptions about human behavior because of an overly simplistic interpretation of Greek philosophy. The Greeks taught us that what people think and feel determines what they do.

These ancient philosophers who have contributed significantly to our thinking were only partly right. While it is true that what we think and feel influences what we do, it is also true that *what we do influences what we think*. Very often, our actions condition our thought patterns and determine our feelings more than we are willing to admit. This fact has great relevance for our discussion on love. It leads us to the important discovery that if we decide to do loving things for people, these actions can generate loving feelings toward those people.

Love as Action

Sometimes in counseling situations, I encounter persons who claim an absence of any kind of affectionate feelings for their mates. These people say that whatever they once felt has died and that they are left with no alternative but to end their marriage. Whenever I counsel such people, I always tell them that if they will do faithfully what I tell them to do, within a month the feelings of affection will return. I tell them that if they follow my directions, they will once again be "in love" with the person to whom they are married. When they ask me if I have some new and secret method to employ, I simply tell them to do the following:

1. Each day make a new list of ten things that you would do for your spouse if you were in love.
2. Then each day, do the ten things that are on that list.

It is as simple as that. There is no secret formula or magical recipe. There is no mysterious process that is the result of extensive research. There is only the age-old truth that those who do loving things will have loving feelings.

A man who took this advice called a friend of mine and told a wonderfully funny story of the consequences. He said, "I usually leave the factory sweating and dirty, but I decided that, if I really loved my wife, I would clean up before I saw her again. So I showered and shaved. I put on clean clothes. On the way home, I stopped at a florist and bought some flowers for her. I usually go in the back door, get a beer out of the refrigerator, go into the rec-room and watch TV until supper. But, because I wanted to do what a lover would do, I went to the front door, rang the doorbell, and waited for my wife to answer. When she opened the door, I held out the flowers and said, 'For you, honey! I love you!' She looked at the flowers, then at me, and then burst into tears. She said, 'I've had a terrible day. Billy broke his leg and I had to take him to the hospital. I no sooner got him home from the hospital than the phone rang. It was your mother. She's coming to visit for two weeks. I tried to do the wash, and the washing machine broke. There's water all over the basement floor. *And now you have to come home drunk!*'"

Nevertheless, if this man keeps on doing such things, I'm sure that it will not be long before his heart is palpitating with excitement over being married. If he does what he promised to do, it's only a matter of time before he will find that his marriage is fun again.

When the Bible tells husbands to love their wives, it is telling them to do those things that lovers do. If husbands obey this admonition, it will not be long before they feel those things that lovers feel. Since this is how the emotions, which are so important to us, come into play, there is little excuse for getting out of a marriage by claiming a loss of love. The deadness of the heart can be taken away. The fervor of passion can be rekindled. The prosaic can become poetic. The mundane can become sublime. All that is needed is a commitment to *do* those things that lovers do. Love is a commitment to do those things for the other person that will help bring to fruition all the fun and happiness that God intends for that person. Such a commitment results in actions which, little by little, generate the "turn-on" that gives life new exhilaration. Such actions result in the emotions that make for the best kind of fun.

I have tried what I am suggesting. I can vouch for the fact that the more I have done loving things for my wife, the more I enjoy her. The more I do what a lover is supposed to do, the more fun we have together. The Greeks were half right. What we think and feel does influence what we do, but what we do influences greatly how we feel.

Listening as Lovers Do

Few things help foster feelings of love as much as listening does. When I say listening, I mean *really* listening, not the kind of half-listening that often goes on between people.

There have been occasions when my wife has talked to me at great length about something that was very important to her. While I nodded and gave her the typical "uh-huh," my mind was on something else. Of all the things that I have done to hurt my wife's feelings, few things have hurt her as much as my failure to really listen to her when she talks to me.

On the other hand, there are times that I give her my fullest attention. I hang on her every word and involve myself intensely in everything that she is saying. On such occasions, I make listening a passionate experience. Listening like this can be an exhausting process, but it does have a fabulous payoff. It not only generates loving feelings in me, but it provides a real "turn-on" for her. There are few things I can do that excite her more about me than listening to her intently and responsively.

When I was a young single pastor at a small church, I came to a most fascinating realization: a good number of the women in my church were falling in love with me. This is not the delusion of an egotist. I am not a handsome guy who sweeps women off their feet. Actually, I have an oversized nose and I was beginning to get bald even then. On occasion, I have even been told that I am an unattractive person. The thing that attracted these women to me was that I really listened to them.

I am convinced that most men in our society turn into clods shortly after marriage. They treat their wives with increasing indifference. They become preoccupied with sports. And, worst of all, they stop listening to their wives. The deadening effect of an absence of attentive listening makes wives very vulnerable to advances from anyone who shows a genuine interest in them.

My seminary counseling courses had trained me to listen with real attention. As I sat in a counseling session for an hour or so while a woman unburdened herself, I came to realize that she in turn was focusing her attention upon me. One woman said to me at the end of such a session, "Pastor, I don't remember the last time I felt like this with a man." I left quickly, a little wiser about the effect that listening can have on a relationship.

Jesus was always using the act of listening in ways that created love and fostered the healing of broken hearts. We read in Chapter 5 of Mark's Gospel of how the Lord faced the demoniac called Legion. Verse 9 tells us how the Lord began His confrontation with this tortured man by asking a simple question: "What is your name?" Jesus had not come to preach. He had come to listen. When His disciples showed up, they found Jesus listening to this man, who by then was "sitting, and clothed, and in his right mind" (v. 15).

Jesus knew the healing power of listening. It is important that we learn something about listening from the one who made love His business. Concentrated listening generates love. It creates love in the listener, and it creates love in the person who has something to share. If the law of Christ is love, then sharing burdens through listening helps us to live out that law. We are told in Galatians 6:2 to bear each other's burdens, and so we should. Listening can make the difference.

The Powerlessness of Love

Willard Wallard, a sociologist who exercised significant influence on American intellectual thought during the first half of this century, discovered that for love to increase in a relationship, power must decrease. Wallard recognized that there was an inverse relationship between love and power, so that when the one increased, the other decreased. He called this "the principle of

WHO SWITCHED THE PRICE TAGS?

least interest." According to Wallard's principle, the person who has the least love and is the least interested in maintaining a relationship exercises the most power and control over the relationship. Conversely, the person who loves the most and is the most interested in keeping the relationship alive is the most vulnerable and has little control over the other person.

This principle can be observed in most marriages. If a husband is not deeply in love with his wife and is not concerned about the survival of the marriage, while his wife desires to keep the marriage alive, he is in a position to control the relationship.

I know of a husband who is having an affair. His wife knows what he is doing but is powerless to stop it. She is desperate to stay married to him and is convinced that, if she can just keep him from leaving, she will be able to get him to love her again. She's caught in the middle— she can't force her husband to end his affair, and he knows she will not leave him no matter what he does.

The same principle can be observed with high school young people. If there is a teenage girl who is not particularly thrilled with her boyfriend, yet has no better options at the time, that girl can exercise great power over her boyfriend. She can treat him like dirt, have him at her beck and call, dismiss him from her presence, and generally dictate the terms of the relationship. She is in a position of power because she is the one least interested in keeping the relationship going.

Most of us have experienced Wallard's principle in our own lives without knowing that it had an official sociological name. Most of us, at one time or another, have felt the pain that comes from loving a person who does not return that love with the same intensity. Most of us know that powerless, vulnerable feeling that comes when we care more about maintaining a relationship than the other person does.

Some of us defend ourselves against such humiliation and hurt by holding back on love. Many a person has learned the hard way that it is dangerous to become involved with another person until that person has proven that the love will be reciprocated in kind. Consequently, we become afraid to let ourselves go in relationships. We become cautious about loving. We learn how to repress our feelings and hold back affection until we are sure of where we stand. We recognize that love makes us vulnerable, and then we become reluctant to take the risks that love requires. We sometimes think that marriage will solve the problem of vulnerability and that, after the ceremony, it will be safe to love. However, many of us learn with great regret that marriage is not necessarily a safe relationship anymore; that even when marriage lasts, it can be a hell of exploitation at the hands of a partner who cares very little and therefore has the greater power.

Power is something that must be surrendered voluntarily if love is to grow. The more that a person is able to set aside power for the sake of love, the more fully love will be expressed. This is best illustrated by Jesus, who, in His desire to express His love for us, was willing to set aside His power, humble Himself, assume the role of a servant, and allow Himself to be put to death.

Let this mind be in you, which was also in Christ Jesus: Who, being in the form of God, thought it not robbery to be equal with God: But made himself of no reputation, and took upon him the form of a servant, and was made in the likeness of men: And being found in fashion as a man, he humbled himself, and became obedient unto death, even the death of the cross (Phil. 2:5–8).

Greater love hath no man than this . . . (John 15:13).

If you are really interested in expressing love, you, like Christ, must learn servanthood. If you want love to flourish, you must not seek to exercise your will over others and insist upon having your own way. If you want to enjoy the fun of being in love, then you must risk making yourself vulnerable, always remembering that only by giving up power can love be increased.

Obviously, this important condition for love flies in the face of the practices of male chauvinists. The male who demands that he be in a position of domination and control, in so doing diminishes his capacity to express love. It is little wonder that so many men in America find it difficult to say the simple words "I love you" in a meaningful way. Expressing love diminishes the power of the male, and, since he is socialized to play power games with women, he is often doomed to a loveless existence.

Once, when I counseled a couple that was having problems, the wife blurted out, "I can't remember the last time he said, 'I love you.'" His retort was, "When I married you twenty-eight years ago, I told you that I loved you, and I said that if I ever changed my mind I'd let you know." This man was more in love with power than he was with his wife. And, until the power of love becomes greater than his love for power, this couple will have little hope for a fulfilling relationship.

What the World Needs Now Is Love, Sweet Love

There are some ardent feminists who also must discover the validity of Wallard's principle. Evangelical Christians so desperately need the insights and truths of the feminist movement that I am reluctant to criticize any of its spokespersons. Nevertheless, if the feminist movement is to achieve its goal of fostering more loving relationships between men and women (and at its best, the feminist movement does have this as its goal), then it must see that women are oppressed, not because they are so self-giving, but because men are on power trips. They are quite right when they call upon us to examine social processes whereby we train boys to be tough, aggressive power-lovers. We must come to see that the more we succeed in training boys to love power, the more we create men who lack the sweet sensitivity, compassion, and humility that are essential for loving. Boys must be taught that women are to be loved rather than controlled. If there is to be hope for the institution of marriage, men must learn that the desire to dominate their wives must be set aside. They must be delivered from the love of power so they can be free to love. Too often, however, the feminists are more concerned about the tendency of women to make themselves vulnerable than they are about the tendency of men to dominate. Vulnerability is good. So is self-sacrifice.

If love is to exist, both the man and the woman must come to the point of "submitting . . . one to another in the fear of God."* Both must learn to outdo one another in service and humility. As Philippians 2:3 tells us, "Let nothing be done through strife or vainglory;

* Eph. 5:21.

but in lowliness of mind let each esteem others better than themselves."

Ideally, marriages should unite people who are prepared to sacrifice for each other. The wife should be saying to her husband, "I am going to sacrifice my life for your well-being. I am going to do everything I can do to help you become all that God wills for you to be. I am ready to sacrifice my own aspirations and dreams for your sake."

In this ideal marriage, the husband will say, in response, "Oh, no! I am going to sacrifice *my* life for *your* well-being. I am going to do everything *I* can do to help *you* to become all *you* can be. I am ready to sacrifice *my* aspirations and dreams for *you.*"

And she responds, "Oh, no! It's the other way around. . . ." And they have their first fight.

It's the only kind of fight that a Christian couple is supposed to have. It is a fight in which each tries to outdo the other in love.

Letting God Love Through You

There is more to becoming a Christian than accepting a set of doctrines and striving to live out a particular lifestyle. Being a Christian involves allowing God to become a living presence in your life. A Christian is a person who is in Christ and in whom Christ dwells. A Christian is a person who is possessed by Christ in such a way that feelings, thoughts, and attitudes are all changed. For the Christian person, loving becomes a spiritual exercise because God is love, and the Christian knows that "every one that loveth is born of God."* God wants to indwell you and affect your consciousness for many reasons, but above them all is His desire to be able to reach other people with His love through you. There is no doubt that Jesus is resurrected from the dead, is with you every moment, and longs for you to invite Him to be a presence in your life. "Behold, I stand at the door . . . ," He says in Revelation 3:20. If you will pray and ask Him to be an indwelling reality and if you are willing to yield to His will in all things, He will enter into your consciousness and begin to effect a transformation in your life. Most important, you will, little by little, begin to relate to other people as He would relate to them. You will recognize that being a Christian involves a commitment to treat others as He would treat them.

What most affected my feelings for others was the strange discovery that the Jesus who loved me and gradually was increasing His presence in my life was waiting to be loved in any person who came into my presence. I am not advocating some monistic or pantheistic philosophy, but since I became a Christian, I have come to see a sacramental meaning in the lives of other people. When I look deeply and intensely into another person's eyes, I often sense the presence of God through that person. When this miracle of grace occurs, it becomes easy to love the other person, sometimes in spite of the fact that the person is behaving in a very unlovable fashion. The ability to love the unlovable, for me, is tied up with a growing sense that the

* 1 John 4:7.

Jesus whom I love bids me to love Him symbolically in the person who confronts me.

No person plays the priestly role of being a conduit through whom Jesus comes to me as much as my wife does. In my relationships with her, I sense in new ways the truth of Matthew 25:40. When I take the time to look into her eyes and enter into the holy of holies of her personhood, I hear a soft, still voice in the depths of my being saying, "What you do and feel for her, you do and feel for Me."

If you want to *do* something that will cause you to become a more loving person, surrender yourself to Jesus. He has a way of making lovers out of people. There is nothing that is of more value than love. There is nothing that brings more enjoyment to life than love. There is nothing that is more fun than love.

Part Four

IN CHURCH LIFE

THE NOW BODY OF CHRIST

Two thousand years ago, the eternal Christ was incarnated in a man named Jesus. The hands of that man Jesus were the hands of God, and with those hands God touched those who had leprosy and made them whole. The feet of that man Jesus were the feet of God, and with those feet God walked among the people of this world so that we might behold God's glory. The tongue of that man Jesus was the tongue of God, and it was with that tongue that God uttered the most important words ever put into human language. Two thousand years ago, Christ who is the eternal Son of God, expressed Himself in a historical human body.

Today, God still seeks to incarnate Himself in human

form. He still endeavors to embody Himself in history. However, the *now* body of Christ is the church, as 1 Corinthians 12 tells us. Jesus Christ, who walked the dusty roads of ancient Palestine, wants to establish His physical presence in today's world through the church. It is through the church that He wants to heal the sick, bring good news to the poor, bring about justice, and declare His gospel. It is through the church that He wills to bring all things into subjection unto Himself as we see in Ephesians 1:20–23.

A small boy, after being tucked into bed for the night, cried out, "Mommy, I'm afraid to be alone in the dark. I want somebody to stay with me."

His mother responded, "Don't be afraid. God is with you."

The little boy then said sadly, "I want somebody with skin on his face."

Through the church, Christ tries to present Himself to our world. Not only did the eternal God reveal Himself in human flesh two thousand years ago, but He seeks to express Himself tangibly in this present time in the church. Men and women who are willing to be His body here and now can be contemporary hands for God to do His work. Those who are willing to be "in Christ" as persons committed to serving Him with the totality of their beings will discover that He is in them. While there will always be a qualitative difference between the only begotten Son of God and those of us whom He chooses to call His brothers, there is a sense in which we who are the church are called to be the incarnation of Christ's love— and, consequently, the *now* body of Christ.

To become Christian is to become committed to the

church. The Roman Catholics have often said that there is no salvation outside the church. While I do not believe that we must or should become part of an ecclesiastical bureaucratic system, I do believe that Christians, by definition, are persons who are bound together in the love of God for the express purpose of incarnating the eternal Christ in our time. Those who think they can be Christians while refusing to participate in the body of Christ deceive themselves. That is the main emphasis of the crucial passage about the church recorded in 1 Corinthians 12:12–15 and 20–21:

> For as the body is one, and hath many members, and all the members of that one body, being many, are one body: so also is Christ. For by one Spirit are we all baptized into one body, whether we be Jews or Gentiles, whether we be bond or free; and have been all made to drink into one Spirit. For the body is not one member, but many. If the foot shall say, Because I am not the hand, I am not of the body; is it therefore not of the body? . . . But now are they many members, yet but one body. And the eye cannot say unto the hand, I have no need of thee: nor again the head to the feet, I have no need of you.

Every once in a while, somebody reminds me that the church is full of hypocrites. In response to such a statement, I say that this is why everyone is welcomed. I have never met a human being who was not a hypocrite. So far as I am concerned the most hypocritical people in the world are those who have been "conned" by their own hypocritical pretenses into believing that they themselves are devoid of hypocrisy. When someone tells me that he or she knows people who are neither Christian nor a part of Christ's church and yet seem to live better lives than some Christians, I like to respond by saying, "If they are so wonderful *without* being 'in Christ,' then think of how much more wonderful they would be if they would trust in Christ and join His church." Then I go on to add, "And if you think I am so hypocritical and phony *with* Christ, can you imagine what I would be like without Him and His church?"

To put a high value on being part of the church is to put a high value on what can bring joy and fulfillment to life. On the day of Pentecost, when the Holy Spirit gave birth to the New Testament church, the people of God were so filled with excitement and joy that onlookers thought they were drunk. But they weren't. They were only experiencing the first real joy—the first real fun—that God had planned for His church.

> But Peter, standing up with the eleven, lifted up his voice, and said unto them, "Ye men of Judea, and all ye that dwell at Jerusalem, be this known unto you, and hearken to my words: For these are not drunken, as ye suppose, seeing it is but the third hour of the day" (Acts 2:14–15).

People who refuse to be part of the church do not have the opportunity to experience the unity, the spiritual energy, and the joy that the Holy Spirit imparts to the body of Christ. If you find no joy in your church, if you find it boring, legalistic, or even contentious, I call upon you to be an agent of God's joy and carry that joy into the body of believers to which you belong. You can make a difference. You can express such joyful vitality that your presence will enliven a dull church until it becomes a true gathering in which joy is contagious. I call upon you to challenge your church to live up to what it can become.

The Church Is the Best Means to Witness for Christ

I recently heard a television preacher say that television is the most effective means presently available for evangelism. He tried to encourage people to make contributions to his ministry by claiming that there is no better means than television to reach the lost masses of humanity with the gospel. Of course that evangelist was wrong. He was not even close to the truth. The best instrument for evangelism is the ordinary church member bearing witness to a vital faith. It always has been; it always will be.

Sometimes when I am trying to impress an audience with this fact, I take a survey by calling for a show of hands in order to learn how the people came to be Christians. In an audience of a thousand people, perhaps one or two raise their hands when I ask how many became Christians because of a television program. When I ask for those who became Christians by reading a gospel tract or listening to a religious radio show, I expect no response. When I ask how many became Christians through evangelistic crusades, I get a limited, but respectable, response. But, when I ask how many became Christians because of persons who loved them and brought them to church, the response is overwhelming.

There is a high probability that if you are a Christian, it is because a member of the church invited you and then some of the people of the church loved you into making a decision for Christ. Generally, people are led into a personal relationship with Christ because there have been church members who cared enough to talk to them and love them into the Kingdom. It is interesting to note that while pastors and preachers are important instruments for the proclamation of the word of God, ordinary lay people are the primary agents for evangelizing the world.

Remember the story I told earlier about the beautiful woman passenger on the plane who shared her faith with "Mr. Cool"? That is the way the Kingdom grows. That is the way the church grows. That is the way the lost are led to Christ. One on one is the best play in the Christian game.

Lay People Are the Church in the World

The church has been ordained to reach the world through lay persons. They are in the best position to carry out God's evangelistic mandate. Professional clergy often find that people outside the church set up barriers that make it very difficult for them to communicate the gospel in an effective manner. During the years when I served as a Baptist pastor, I found that people tended to become artificial in my presence. When I went into the barber shop one day, the barber said, "Good afternoon," in a normal tone and then shouted, "REVEREND!" The moment he said the word *Reverend*, everybody in the barber shop froze. *Playboy* magazines were shoved out of sight, people smiled self-consciously, and inane conversations hastily began.

"Nice weather we're having," said one man.

"Yeah, I'm glad it didn't snow," said another.

Everybody became phony in the presence of the

Reverend. The artificial atmosphere created by my presence made it impossible for me to talk to them about the gospel and the really meaningful things in their lives.

The laity does not experience this problem. The barriers that clergy encounter outside the church do not exist for them. The non-Christian community is more open to people who are not identified as religious professionals.

Of course, there are those who claim that "only those who walk the walk can talk the talk." By this, they mean that if Christians do not live in a manner consistent with their message, they will not get a fair hearing from others with whom they share the gospel. Our lifestyle as Christians should be a testimony to the validity of our message, but if we had to be spiritually perfect in order to witness for Christ, no one would qualify. In his letter to the Philippians, the Apostle Paul responded to those who claimed that only the spiritually perfect could be effective witnesses by saying, "Not that I . . . am already perfected; but I press on . . . toward the goal for the prize of the upward call of God in Christ Jesus."[*] According to Paul, we must share the gospel while we are still in the process of changing into truly Christianized people. He wanted us to know that if we wait until we are the kind of people we ought to be before witnessing, we will never get the evangelistic job done. As imperfect people who are heirs to the grace of God, we are called to invite people to join us as we strive together to become more and more like Christ.

[*] Phil. 3:12–14, NKJV.

Lack of Perfection Is No Excuse

While serving as a pastor, I had a tendency to alienate the people of my church with caustic one-liners. Needless to say, such quips did not make for successful pastoring.

On one occasion, I asked a man in my church if he would be willing to be a teacher for a Sunday School class of junior high school boys. The man very piously held his oversized Bible over his heart and whined, "Oh, Pastor! I'd love to teach that class. Only the Lord knows how much I'd enjoy sharing the Word with those precious little lads, but, Pastor, . . . I'm so unworthy. I'm so undeserving."

Before I could catch myself I said, "I know! If we had anybody better, do you think we'd ask you?"

That was hardly a diplomatic or Christian remark, but I'm sure there are countless numbers of pastors who feel like doing the same thing when they face similar circumstances. Declarations of inadequacy, which often are feigned rather than real, are a commonly used means of escaping from Christian service. We should do our best to prevent such evasions of Christian responsibility. God can draw straight lines with crooked sticks. God can use imperfect persons to do His perfect will. The effectiveness of our service is more dependent upon what God is than upon what we are. In spite of all our shortcomings, we still remain the primary means through which Christ seeks to share His message with the lost and to transform His world into what He wills for it to be.

The Renaissance scholar Erasmus, endeavoring to emphasize the importance of carrying out the evangelistic mandate, once told a most interesting story. In his mythical tale, Jesus returns to heaven after His time on earth. The angels gather around Him to learn of the events that occurred during the days of the Incarnation. Jesus tells them of His miracles, His teachings, His death, His resurrection and, finally, He tells them about His ascension to heaven. When He finishes His story, Michael the Archangel asks, "But Lord, what happens now?"

Jesus answers, "I have left behind eleven faithful men who will declare My message and express My love. These faithful men will build My church."

"But," responds Michael, "what if these men fail? What then?"

In a slow and thoughtful manner, Jesus answers, "I have no other plan."

For better or for worse, we who are now members of the body of Christ are the instruments God has chosen to spread His word and build His Kingdom.

There are those who agree that the world should be won to Christ by ordinary Christians but who are quick to claim that we should avoid any direct presentation of the gospel. These critics of straightforward witnessing claim that if we live out the message of the Bible, it is unnecessary for us to preach to people. They claim that if our lives are what they should be, people will want to be Christians simply because of the influence we exert through our lifestyle.

I really doubt that there are many people asking such Christians about the message of Jesus. Actually, I think most people are put off by those who represent themselves as being better than others. Furthermore, I doubt that many Christians have a lifestyle so consistent that others are impressed enough to want to be converted. I am almost afraid that if people get too close to me, they will discover my inconsistencies and recognize the hypocrisy that is all too evident in my everyday life. When I am behind the pulpit, pontificating about the way in which Christians should live, I may sound like a "super Christian," but in day-to-day living my flaws and failures become all too apparent. I am committed to becoming more like Jesus every day, but I recognize that it would be arrogant to suggest that a close examination of my life would reveal enough purity and goodness to warrant close imitation, or even enough to perfectly represent my Lord. I preach a lifestyle that is better than the one I live. I am open to the Holy Spirit who daily assists me in trying to live a more consistent Christian life, but because I am not yet perfected in Christ, I will continue to declare Him and not myself.

The "Whosoever Will Come" Crowd

My wife sometimes says jokingly that the church is the light of the world, and like all lights, it attracts bugs. Needless to say, she does not believe that people can be thought of as "bugs." All she suggests with her humor is that many people come to the church who would not be attracted to or be accepted by any other group. The reason that so many strange and "irregular people" are found in the church is that such people often recognize that they will find more acceptance there than in any other gathering of people.

I do not accept the idea that churches are just social clubs that are closed to people who are not deemed "proper." I have seen too many churches that readily accept and love people who would be rejected in any other setting. Certainly, there are exclusive-minded churches that ostracize those who fail to measure up to their standards of social acceptability. But in the overwhelming number of cases, churches distinguish themselves by being capable of accepting the socially unacceptable. Of course, there are blatant examples of how certain churches have closed their doors to Black people, but there are also countless cases wherein church members have committed themselves completely to affirming the oneness of all people in Christ. I have seen churches composed primarily of conventional, middle-class people lovingly accept long-haired hippies. I have seen churches where educated and sophisticated members affectionately embrace the poor. I know churches that welcome into their worship services schizophrenic street people and tolerate their disturbing behavior without so much as a thought of asking them to leave.

Even those who criticize churches that ostracize people in an un-Christlike manner recognize that such cases do not reflect what the church is really all about. By pointing to the exceptions, they only validate the claim that the normative attitude of the church is one of acceptance.

I am not trying to justify the church. Anyone who is as much involved with churches as I am knows that most Christians have a long, long way to go to become what Christ expects them to be. Nevertheless, churches do better than most social groups when it comes to being open and accepting.

For all of their weaknesses, most churches are still bodies of believers striving to be as accepting as their

Lord. Those who join in their activities can usually attest to the fact that one of the best aspects of being the body of Christ is getting to know all kinds of people from all kinds of backgrounds.

When churches violate this principle of Christian hospitality, they are likely to receive the strongest condemnation, not from the world, but from other churches who are embarrassed by such behavior. This is especially true when churches practice racial discrimination. Most churches, for instance, readily condemn the churches of South Africa for their support of apartheid.

Even among Christians who have strong feelings against homosexual behavior, there is general agreement that homosexuals themselves must be accepted by the body of believers and loved as brothers and sisters in Christ. For all of its flaws and shortcomings, the *now* body of Christ is made up of people who are endeavoring to be as accepting of those whom the world generally rejects as was the *then* body of Christ two thousand years ago.

A few years ago I was asked to be a speaker at a very affluent and very formal Presbyterian church located just outside Washington, D.C. The worship service that Sunday proceeded with all the dignity that expresses Presbyterianism at its best. The magnificent sanctuary, the stately music, and the properly attired congregation blended together to give the impression that all things were being done "decently and in order."

Quite unexpectedly, the decorum of the church was disrupted by a barefooted young man who was spaced-out on drugs and dressed in rags. This disreputable-looking creature stumbled down the main aisle of the church all the way to the front of the sanctuary. The entire congregation was taken aback by the intruder. I watched with much anxiety as he stood and stared at the preacher. Then, suddenly, he squatted on the floor just to the right of the pulpit.

The pastor tried to ignore him and did his best to keep the service moving along, but he was obviously upset. Then a tall, elderly gentleman, dressed in establishment attire, got up from his pew and walked deliberately down the aisle toward the strange visitor. The old man carried a brass-capped cane, and some feared that he was going to use it to drive the hippie intruder out of the sanctuary. But instead, something remarkable happened. The old man paused beside that dirty and ragged young man, sat down, and put his arm around his shoulder. Those unlikely partners sat arm in arm for the rest of the service. They provided the congregation of that church with the real sermon of the morning.

The loving acceptance of church people has always been a primary factor in winning people to Christ. Very often, it is this love more than anything else that leads people to become Christians. Over and over again people attest to the fact that it was not the piety but the love they found in the church that moved them to consider making a serious commitment to Christ. No wonder ordinary church people are more effective in the work of evangelism than all the television evangelists put together!

Making Church Fun

I have not yet addressed the fact that, for many people, church services are boring. If we are honest, many of us will admit that the eleven o'clock hour on Sunday is not the most interesting time of the week. When our children complain that they do not want to go to church because it's no fun, they draw more sympathy from us than we want to admit.

A great deal of the blame for the tedious character of many worship services lies with those who lead them. If more of the clergy took worship seriously, I am certain that the attitude of many people toward churchgoing could be greatly improved.

A friend of mine who teaches in a theological seminary complained to me recently that his students did not deem what happens in worship services to be of crucial significance to the overall ministry of the church. My friend reported that his students believed counseling, social action programs, and pastoral visitation to be more important than worship. These students put great emphasis upon preaching and were convinced that what they had to say to their people in sermons was the most important part of the worship hour. But for most of them, the rest of the service was inconsequential. My friend pointed out that his students considered what went before the sermon to be relatively unimportant.

Some pastors think that their homilies are all that matter. They sometimes forget that the primary reason for the gathering of the saints is the worship of God.

A friend of mine visited a neighborhood church in her community. After the service, as she was leaving the sanctuary, one of the older women of the church stopped her for some friendly talk and visiting. While they were talking, the eight-year-old son of the pastor climbed into the pulpit and shouted over the public address system,

"Look everybody! Look at me! I'm in the pulpit." The elderly woman to whom my friend was speaking remarked coldly, "His father preaches that every Sunday."

When a pastor uses morning worship services to bring glory to himself or herself rather than to God, church ceases to be fun for anyone. Every minister of the gospel who conducts worship owes it to the congregation to plan the services to focus on the Lord. The prayers should be carefully structured to express with beauty, as well as with sincerity, the heartfelt longings of those who come seeking a time with God. The hymns should be thoughtfully chosen to communicate the theme of the service and to lift the spirits of the saints to the throne of grace. Those who lead in worship should spend hours in planning and prayer, recognizing that in true worship God is the audience, the members of the congregation are the performers, and the person in the pulpit is the prompter.

We make a mistake, however, if we think that the professionals who are our pastors ultimately determine what happens to us in a worship service. The congregation has more to do with what goes on during the worship hour than most people recognize.

First of all, the people in the pews set the tone for worship. There are some congregations that bring into worship a contagious joy that creates a good feeling even before the first hymn is sung or the first prayer is said. As a visiting preacher, I have taken my place on many a pulpit chair and immediately sensed an enthusiastic expectancy from the people who waited for me to lead them in worship. Their joy and aliveness on such occasions gave me a confidence that insured their getting the best I had to offer. I have found that often the spirit with which people approach the singing of hymns can set the tone for the service. And most of all, I have found that the friendliness of a congregation can be of vital importance. In churches where I have found people visiting happily with each other and expressing genuine gladness to be together, the hour of worship has been an hour of holy fun. The attitude of the congregation can contribute toward making church services more exciting than the most gifted of preachers.

As I mentioned, I belong to a large inner-city church. The membership of our church is over two thousand, and more than a thousand people can be expected to show up for Sunday morning worship. You can imagine my surprise when, upon the death of the pastor who had led our congregation for almost forty years, the pulpit committee selected as our new pastor a young man who had just graduated from seminary. When I heard this news, I sought out the chairperson of the pulpit committee and let him know, in no uncertain terms, that I thought that the committee had made a mistake. I explained that a church as large and as prestigious as ours needed someone who was established as a great preacher. The elderly chairman of the pulpit committee smiled and responded with these memorable words: "Tony, we're goin' to make him great." And they did. Their enthusiasm, support, and prayer for that young preacher have lifted him to a level of greatness that most preachers never reach.

Our church is a fun place to be. There is a happiness in the congregation. There is a sense that people are glad to be there. We are known as a hugging and kissing church. Sometimes visitors cannot figure us out because we are having such fun together. Furthermore, I am convinced that Jesus really enjoys being with us on Sunday mornings.

Abraham Lincoln once said that people are usually just about as happy as they make up their minds to be. I believe the same is true of churches. The congregations of churches are just as happy as they decide to be. You can *decide* to make your church a happy place. If you place a high value on making worship fun (the more pious term is "joyful"), it will happen. If you do not— well, you can guess what will occur at the eleven o'clock hour on Sunday morning. It just might be the dullest hour of the week.

THE WAY THE CHURCH HAS FUN

The church puts a high value on service. Its members have been taught that they serve their master by serving others. They know that Jesus has a special commitment to the poor and the oppressed, and they, in turn, are committed to following His example. They constantly hear His words ringing in their ears: "Inasmuch as ye have done it unto one of the least of these my brethren, ye have done it unto me."*

There are those pseudo-sophisticated members of the secular intelligentsia who endeavor to demonstrate their comprehension of world history and cultural anthropology

*Matt. 25:40.

by bad-mouthing the church and deriding its missionary endeavors. They snidely suggest that the world would be better off if missionaries stayed home and let the "primitive" peoples of the world live in the simplicity of their unspoiled cultures. Of course, such uninformed critics ignore the fact that many of those so-called wholesome native customs which the missionaries disrupted involved child sacrifice, slavery, and cannibalism. These heirs of Rousseau usually forget that those "simple primitives" often lived in the context of animistic religions which terrorized them with fears of evil spirits. They've read just enough of James Michener's *Hawaii* to be dangerous, generalizing the bad rap Michener gave some missionaries to condemn all who have tried to be modern-day apostles of love and service.

Whatever mistakes missionaries may have made in their attempts to communicate the gospel crossculturally, there is little question that they were motivated by love and concern rather than by economic and commercial interests. Anyone who has witnessed the impact of raw capitalism unaccompanied by missionary love quickly realizes that missionaries provide the best kind of initial encounter with non-Western cultures. People in the Two-Thirds Nations resent the exploitation of American business interests much more than they deprecate the service of missionaries. When missionaries are asked to leave their fields of service, it is usually because, in the minds of the native people, they are too closely allied with Western economic and political interests.

The Way the Church Has Fun

A Story about William and Joanna Hodges

There is a hospital in Limbe, Haiti, which is run by William and Joanna Hodges, an American Baptist couple. These dedicated medical missionaries have faithfully served over 450,000 Haitian people with love and respect for almost forty years. In any given year, Dr. and Mrs. Hodges care for over 95,000 patients. They provide the only care for diabetics in the northern part of the country, and they are the only ones who give protection to those mentally ill men and women who the native voodoo witch doctors claim are possessed by evil spirits.

When I visited in the summer of '86, I found two incredible people who had become joyfully imprisoned by their love for the Haitian people. It had been more than twenty years since they had made a visit home to the United States. Airplanes, piloted by missionaries of the Missionary Aviation Fellowship, make daily runs from their part of Haiti to Fort Lauderdale, Florida, but these two devoted Christians love their patients too much to leave them even for a short visit to their homeland. "How can we leave?" asks William Hodges. "Early every morning, hundreds of patients line up waiting for help. I just can't go off and leave them. I'm trapped here," he says with a laugh. He does not even leave the mission hospital for R & R breaks in the cities of Haiti. When I spoke with him, it had been eight years since he had been to Port-au-Prince, the capital, and almost four years since he had visited Cap-Haitien, the second largest city of the country, which is located only twenty miles down the road from his hospital at Limbe.

For fun, William Hodges works as a brilliant amateur archeologist. His museum, perhaps the most important in the Caribbean, displays an amazing array of artifacts that tell the story of Haiti's fascinating past. His love for the Haitian people is evidenced in his respect for their history and the care that he gives to displaying the elements of their culture.

I visited the hospital at Limbe just after a revolution in Haiti had toppled the oppressive rule of the Duvalier family. There had been a breakdown of law and order, and many Americans were taking advantage of any available opportunity to slip out of the country. As Dr. Hodges and I crossed the road that separated his museum from his medical complex, we were intercepted by two Haitian women who called to us in Creole, "You do not think you can leave us, do you? We will not let you leave. You are our doctor. You belong to us. If you try to leave, many people will block your way."

"I'm going to leave; just you wait and see," he said jokingly.

"No! You cannot!" they shouted back at him. "We will not let you. We love you too much to let you go."

The Sacredness of Life in a Desperate World

Haiti is a place permeated by poverty. As in all poor countries, death is accepted as an everyday occurrence. In such a place, it would be easy to get the idea that life is not precious, but the Christian influence of William and Joanna Hodges has kept this from happening. One day, as I toured the bleak wards of the Limbe Hospital, I

184

saw an amazing example of how precious life can be for those who are in Christ.

In one of the wards, seated cross-legged on her bed, I found a hydrocephalic girl. The brain of this unfortunate young person had been compressed by the accumulation of fluid in her skull, and, for almost all of her thirteen years of existence, she had sat on that bed nervously rocking her deformed body. The Christian Haitian nurses of Limbe changed her diapers many times a day, using precious minutes that might have been given to more hopeful patients. Nevertheless, day after day, week after week, and year after year, these nurses cleaned up the messes made by this brain-damaged child, and they did so without complaint.

One day, this hydrocephalic girl accidentally rocked her way to the edge of her bed and crashed to the cement floor. She was seriously hurt and, for a while, it seemed as though the fall would prove fatal. But her nurses would not let her die. It seemed to me that those nurses would have welcomed the death of one who could easily be categorized as a worthless bother. I would have expected them to greet the accident with pious platitudes about its being God's will. Such was not the case. Those tired, overworked nurses gathered around that suffering child and prayed long and hard for her recovery. They lovingly cared for her and gave her back the life she had almost lost. Through it all, the nurses made one thing obvious—for them, life was sacred. Their treatment of that hydrocephalic girl was the antithesis of the World War II concentration camp mentality displayed at Auschwitz. Those nurses were a contradiction of that form of Social Darwinism that deems it better to leave "inferior" forms of life to die. The message of a Christ who is alive in "the least" of persons was too much a part of the world-view of those nurses to allow them to turn off their love for a child whom many would find worthless.

Stories of missionaries like Dr. and Mrs. Hodges abound. There are more of them than the critics of the church would want to count. A complete survey of missionary work around the world would reveal that Mother Teresa is not quite the exception that the media pretend she is. There are thousands of Mother Teresas who humbly carry out the mission of the church. Without benefit of TV coverage or Nobel Prizes, they do their work in obscurity. I find the glib criticisms of missionary work much less than amusing.

The Church and the Cherokees

Some years ago, I was chosen to serve a one-year term as a vice president of the American Baptist Convention. That year my denomination held its annual convention in Minneapolis, Minnesota, and I was privileged to preside over several of the sessions. One day while I was conducting the business of the convention, the proceedings were disrupted by the intrusion of a group of angry American Indians. They took control of the convention and, once in charge, condemned what the "whites" had done to the Indians over the years. They accused the audience of being racists who had mistreated native Americans. They poured out pronouncements of hatred for white people and vowed to throw off the yoke of white enslavement.

Their presence and statements went unchallenged until they started to level specific charges against Christianity and the church. At that point, a single voice of opposition was heard from among the thousands gathered in the auditorium. It was the voice of a young Cherokee Indian woman. She rose to her feet, made her way to the platform, and took the microphone away from the Indian chief who was the primary spokesperson for the group. Then, in an unforgettable speech, she pleaded her case, claiming that whatever evils whites had brought upon the American Indians, the church was not one of them. She described the history of the Cherokee Indians and gave special attention to the events that surrounded the "Trail of Tears," their historic journey from their homeland in Georgia to the barren spaces of Oklahoma. She explained how Andrew Jackson had called for the removal of the Cherokees from their ancient tribal lands and designated a new home for them where they would not be in the way of "white" economic interests. She pointed out that only a handful of whites had stood up to President Jackson and challenged his unjust and deplorable actions.

"It was the missionaries," she said, "who took our case before the Supreme Court. It was the missionaries, who, when they were unable to stop what the government willed for the Cherokees, took their stand with them and walked the long walk halfway across the continent."

She went on to explain how hundreds of Indians had died on that march to the Oklahoma dust bowl which was to be their new home. And then she explained that among those who had died in the "Trail of Tears" were Baptist missionaries who had chosen to identify with their oppressed Indian friends. "But that is not the end of the story," she said. "After the Cherokees arrived in Oklahoma, they chose some of their strongest braves and sent them back to Georgia to dismantle the little chapel where their missionaries had once worshiped. The braves were instructed to carry the pieces of the chapel back to their new home in Oklahoma where they could be assembled for the worship of God."

When she finished her speech, a hushed silence fell over the thousands assembled in the municipal forum. There were tears in the eyes of the Indian braves who stood by her side. They knew that while the history of whites in general had been despicable, the history of the Church was made of better stuff. The Church deserved more credit than they had given it.

Service Is the Joy of the Church

Church people owe service to Christ and His world. After all that He has done and is doing for us, the least we can do is to offer ourselves for service to Him. Self-sacrifice is the only reasonable response to the mercies of God. As we read in Romans 12:1, we are urged "by the mercies of God, that [we] present [our] bodies a living sacrifice, holy, acceptable unto God, which is [our] reasonable service." While there is something to be admired in those who grit their teeth and make themselves do what has to be done in the name of Jesus, for many Christians, service is rendered to others for less noble reasons. When really pressed, they are likely to admit that their service in the name of Christ is often rendered because they have found that serving others is *fun*.

None of us can imagine Mother Teresa waking up in the morning and saying to herself, "Well, here goes another rotten day on the stinking streets of Calcutta." We know that she has discovered something that may seem like "foolishness to the world" (1 Cor 2:14). She has found the joy that comes from encountering the Jesus in the suffering people she serves each day of her life.

I have a hard time understanding why so many people buy into a cultural value system that promises fun and fulfillment to those who achieve positions of wealth and prestige. So many of these "successes" have broken marriages, are hooked on drugs, are under psychiatric care, or are seeking nirvana in such philosophies as est that this value system should certainly be called into question. How many establishment executives, lawyers, doctors, and accountants have to decry the emptiness of their lives before this generation of young people stops thinking that the "successes" of our society are having fun? How much boredom must egoists who live for themselves exhibit before today's Ivy League preppies realize that Ayn Rand's materialist philosophy of life has holes in it?

On the other hand, I wonder how many missionaries have to tell of the joys of service before their vocation becomes attractive to our young people. How many people like Millard Fuller of Habitat for Humanity must describe the satisfaction they've gained by giving away their money to help poor people before the yuppie owners of Golden American Express cards catch onto the fact that there is more fun in giving than in getting? Why don't they understand how Jimmy Carter, working with Habitat for Humanity, can get more kicks out of fixing up dilapidated housing for welfare families than from the power of the presidency?

There is much evidence that self-giving is what really makes people happy, but somehow most people ignore this evidence and allow themselves to be seduced by our society's false values. Empirical evidence abounds to show that we have been created to render service to others. And yet most Americans choose to ignore that evidence and live primarily for themselves. In saddening reality, most people reject the ways in which God has ordained that we have fun.

We Have a God Who Loves Fun

When my son was nine years old, I took him to Coney Island. I wanted him to see something of the faded glory of what once had been the best of all amusement parks. Together we rode every ride that was still in operation. We tried the ferris wheel and "The Whip." All afternoon, we laughed and screamed until, exhausted, I told him that it was time for us to head home.

"I want one more ride on the roller coaster," he pleaded.

I rejected his plea, but he did not give up.

"Look," he said, "I think Jesus wants me to go on that ride one more time."

That's a new approach, I thought to myself. "Where did you come up with that idea?" I asked him.

"Well," he said, "in your sermons, you say that whatever we feel, Jesus feels. You say that when we are sad, Jesus is sad. And I just thought that if Jesus feels what we feel, then when I am having a good time, so is He.

And I think *He* would like another ride on the roller coaster."

I do not want to construct a Biblical justification for my son's theology, but I have to admit that there is some truth to what he said. If Jesus is in us sharing our emotions and if He is empathetic with our feelings, it only follows that He has a vested interest in our happiness. We can surmise that the more we enjoy life, the more He enjoys life. It may be that this is what lies behind His plan. That is why He calls us to serve others in His name. This may be why He invites us to give our time and energy to His work in the world. Perhaps He prescribes sacrifice and service for us because He knows that sacrifice and service give us the joy that gives Him pleasure.

As you may recall, the movie *Becket* was set in medieval England. Thomas à Becket and King Henry II lived the lives of playboys, womanizing and partying continually. The leaders of the church were critical of the king, not only for his libertine lifestyle, but also for his abuse of power. Upon the death of the Archbishop of Canterbury, the king saw his chance to rid himself of this troublesome criticism by appointing his friend Becket to the post of archbishop. However, upon assuming that role, Becket underwent a change of character. This one-time playboy had resisted being appointed to this high church office, but when ordained he undertook his duties with saintly dedication.

In the scene that most impressed me, Becket, as part of his investiture as archbishop, was required to give away all of his worldly possessions to the poor. The destitute of the community were gathered in the cathedral as the man who was to become their archbishop distributed wealth and personal possessions among them. Suddenly, Becket stopped and turned toward the front of the cathedral. He pointed at the image of Jesus and shouted, "You! Only you know! Only you know how easy this is."

That, of course, is exactly what the world refuses to believe. They see the requirements of discipleship as arduous and are afraid that the religious life is devoid of fun. They are convinced that to be spiritual is to be somber and are threatened by what appears to be a yoke that is too heavy to bear. They refuse to believe that there is joy in self-giving. They refuse to listen to the words of Jesus who said: "Take my yoke upon you, and learn of me; for I am meek and lowly in heart: and ye shall find rest unto your souls. For my yoke is easy and my burden is light."° They fail to understand that the gospel is a contradiction of the wisdom of this world.

Our God Loves Parties

One of the most happy discoveries about God that can come from Bible study is the discovery that God *requires* His people to enjoy themselves and to have parties. If you carefully scrutinize Deuteronomy 14:22–27, you will learn that God commanded the children of Israel to set aside one-tenth of their wealth each year to be used to celebrate His presence among them. In that passage, God ordered His people to bring their tithes to Jerusalem and to use them to finance a huge party in His name. That's right—a party. One-tenth of the wealth of Israel was to be used for an annual celebration. Everybody was invited

°Matt. 11:29–30.

to this party—the rich and the poor; the holy and the sinners; the village drunks and the village rabbis; the "in" crowd and the social rejects; the lame and the blind. No one was to be excluded; all were to be welcomed. Once a year, it was feast time in Jerusalem and once a year, the people of God turned out for a "blow-out" good time. There was to be singing, dancing, and laughter galore. It is no wonder that the boys and girls of ancient Israel joyfully shouted, "I was glad when they said unto me, let us go unto the house of the Lord."

Who would not be glad to go to God's party? A God who enjoys throwing parties obviously is a God who enjoys having His people enjoy themselves. Who can resist loving a God like that?

An Application of the Tithing Principle

God actually puts limits on our giving. He tells us in His Word not to get so carried away with our response to the poor that we forget to do a little partying ourselves.

"Set aside ten percent for the good time," He tells us, "and when you throw your parties, really make them fun. Be sure to invite people who do not deserve to come. Go out into the highways and byways and round up everybody you can. My party is to be an expression of My grace. My party is to be a foretaste of heaven. My party is to be a glimpse of what life will be like when My Kingdom comes to earth. Soup kitchens are good and necessary, but My Kingdom is basically a party."

We need that word. If we forget to set aside ten percent of our assets for partying, we might begin to lose the joy of giving. If we give and give and never have a dime to see a good movie or go on a picnic, we can become resentful of those who do. People who do not party become the grouches who mumble about spend-thrifts who waste money. They are the ones who join ranks with Jesus but get upset whenever others give spontaneous expression to the joy in their hearts.

Then took Mary a pound of ointment of spikenard, very costly, and anointed the feet of Jesus, and wiped his feet with her hair: and the house was filled with the odour of the ointment. Then saith one of his disciples, Judas Iscariot, Simon's son, which should betray him, Why was not this ointment sold for three hundred pence, and given to the poor? This he said, not that he cared for the poor; but because he was a thief, and had the bag, and bare what was put therein. Then said Jesus, Let her alone: against the day of my burying hath she kept this. For the poor always ye have with you; but me ye have not always (John 12:3–8).

Give! Give! Give! Give! But do not forget to set aside a tithe to party with God. We must take the other nine-tenths of what we have and ask God for direction in spending those resources the way He wants. From the nine-tenths we must feed the hungry, clothe the naked, and provide healing for the sick. But we must not forget to set something aside for partying with God. Get an organ for the church. Put up a stained glass window now and then. Just don't get carried away with partying with God; remember that there are limits to the party. There is ten percent for the party, but the rest is to be carefully used to meet our family needs and to meet the needs of others.

Every church needs to make sure it has its values straight. Churches should be filled with celebration, but every church should also be marked by its sacrifices for the oppressed. Each and every church should offer its members the fun of a party, but should also teach about the cheerfulness that comes from meeting the needs of a desperate world.

Loving People Is Fun for Christians

Of all the lessons which the church, at its best, tries to teach its people, the most important is that we should view people as Jesus views them. When church people learn to do this, they will know how to enjoy people in the best possible way.

In an earlier book I told about an incident that happened when I was teaching sociology at the University of Pennsylvania. I had been assigned a course entitled Social Problems, and in that course, we reviewed a variety of the pathologies of society ranging from alcoholism to child abuse.

One day, in order to get class discussion going, I asked my students what some of the world's great religious leaders might have said about prostitution. I asked what Buddha might have said on this subject. I asked what the views of Muhammad might have been. I asked what the Mosaic Law had to say about this dehumanizing practice. The discussion was lively and intense. I was setting the class up to evangelize, and when I felt the time was ripe, I asked what seemed to me to be the crucial question: "What do you suppose Jesus would have said to a prostitute?"

I was all primed to point out to the class the compassion and understanding which Jesus had for the colorful women of the night. I was all set to do my best to make Jesus look greater than all the religious leaders put together. Once again, I asked, "What would Jesus have said to a prostitute?"

One of my Jewish students answered, "Jesus never met a prostitute."

I jumped at the opening; here was my chance, I thought. I could show this guy a thing or two about Jesus and about the New Testament. "Yes, He did," I responded. "I'll show you in my Bible where—"

The young man interrupted me. "You didn't hear me, Doctor. I said Jesus never met a prostitute."

Once again I protested. Once again I reached for my New Testament. I started to leaf through the pages of my Bible searching for those passages which showed Jesus forgiving the "fallen woman." I searched for the place where He gave the woman at the well a chance for spiritual renewal.

Once again, my Jewish student spoke out, this time with a touch of anger in his raised voice. "You're not listening to me, Doctor. You aren't listening to what I am saying. I am saying that Jesus never met a prostitute. Do you think that when he looked at Mary Magdelene he saw a prostitute? Do you think he saw whores when he looked at women like her? Doctor, listen to me! Jesus never met a prostitute!"

I fell silent. My theology was under judgment. I was being corrected by a Jewish student who, in some ways, may have understood Jesus better than some of us who go by the name Christian.

To be a Christian is to learn to see people as Christ sees them. In the church, when the church is really being the church, its members accept things that the world cannot accept. The prostitute becomes a sister. The corrupt politician becomes a brother. The homosexual becomes a fellow saint. The drug addict becomes a priest in the priesthood of all believers.

"Crazy!" you say? Of course it's crazy. At its best, there is no fellowship on earth that is crazier than the church. At its best, the church befriends people we would never get to meet within the sterile confines of our class-structured society. In the church, we are ushered into loving relationships with people who otherwise would be strangers. In the church, Democrats can get to know Republicans, pacifists can get to know soldiers, punk-rockers can get to know lovers of Bach. With that kind of variety, the church has got to be fun.

SOME CLOSING PARAGRAPHS

Just a few closing words to wrap up my case.
My thesis has been a simple one: people everywhere want to have fun, but many do not know how to do it. I have pointed out that people put a lot of stock in things that do not provide a very good pay-off in fun and that they undervalue those things which can deliver the joy and fulfillment that they crave. I have argued that people with mixed-up values cannot have fun because they do not know what will make them happy. I have contended that Jesus felt sorry for us, so He came into our world to forgive us our stupid sins and to straighten out our distorted value systems. He came to teach us about the things that make for joyful living.

However, there is no way to understand Jesus' value system without thinking as He thinks. And there is no way of learning to think as He thinks without asking Him to be with us and in us every moment of every day.

The same Jesus who died on the cross two thousand years ago has been resurrected from the grave. He is right there with you even as you read these lines, and He wants to be *your* personal friend forever. He is a personal Presence who wants to influence the way you think and feel. You can talk to Him and He will listen. He wants to talk to you about things that reallly matter. And though you probably will not hear His words with your ears, if you allow yourself to become very still, you will sense yourself being addressed in the depths of your being.

Until you are personally involved with Jesus, you will not fully understand His value system. And until you understand His value system, you will not know where the fun is. The truth is this: Jesus knows how to live life to the fullest, and if you want to know His secret, you have to get to know Him.

Why not do it? Why not pray, "Jesus, I believe you are here. I want You to forgive me of my sins and make me a new person. But even more, I want You to be a Presence in my life helping me to live life more abundantly."

THE DREAM
Keith Miller

In the Dream, Keith Miller invites us to go on an imaginative journey with him to try to look at ourselves and the church the way God might look at us.

It is not always a happy journey. In many ways, the story shows, we in God's church have let Him down – failing to love and forgive one another, by failing to reach outside ourselves and help those who are in need.

The book is pervaded with a sense of the Lord's sadness and righteous anger over these sins. But it also shines with His overwhelming love, concern and forgiveness. It is fundamentally, a book of hope.

ISBN 0-85009-061-X

YOU CAN MAKE A DIFFERENCE
Tony Campolo

This book challenges young people to make their lives count for Christ. Tony Campolo uniquely identifies with young people in their own situation, then shows how they can use the power of God to change their world. With his incomparable blend of humour and serious biblical insights, the author deals with commitment, vocation, dating and discipleship.

ISBN 0-85009-056-3

PRAYER: KEY TO REVIVAL
Paul Y Cho with R. Whitney Manzano

The secret behind the growth of the largest church in the world!

'No man can schedule a revival', Dr Cho has said, 'for God alone is the giver of life. But . . . when 'the fullness of time' is come and prayer ascends from a few earnest hearts, then history teaches it is time for the tide of revival to sweep in once more.'

This perspective is born of Dr Cho's conviction that while revival is the sovereign work of the Holy Spirit, the earnest prayers of God's people must work with the Spirit. It is then that He moves anew in the hearts of unbelievers.

ISBN 0-85009-059-8

For further details of Word products please complete coupon below.

Books <input type="checkbox" />

Word Records – Cassettes <input type="checkbox" />

Lifelifter Cassettes <input type="checkbox" />

Video <input type="checkbox" />

Please tick items of interest

Name..

Address...

....

....

Word Publishing
Word (UK) Ltd
9 Holdom Avenue, Bletchley, Milton Keynes.
MK1 1QU